retouching photos
in photoshop
elements 3

Visual QuickProject Guide

by Nolan Hester

Peachpit
Press

Visual QuickProject Guide

Retouching Photos in Photoshop Elements 3

Nolan Hester

Peachpit Press

1249 Eighth Street
Berkeley, CA 94710
510/524-2178
800/283-9444
510/524-2221 (fax)

Find us on the World Wide Web at: www.peachpit.com
To report errors, please send a note to errata@peachpit.com
Peachpit Press is a division of Pearson Education

Editor: Nancy Davis
Production Coordinator: David Van Ness
Compositor: David Van Ness
Indexer: Julie Bess
Cover design: The Visual Group with Aren Howell
Interior design: Elizabeth Castro
Interior photos: Nolan Hester (except as noted in Special Thanks on page iv)
Cover photo credit: Getty One

Notice of Rights

Notice of Liability

Trademarks

ISBN – 0-321-32118-9

9 8 7 6 5 4 3 2 1

Printed and bound in the United States of America

This one's for Laika, a true-eyed soul.

Special Thanks to...

Nancy Davis, my beyond-the-call editor, wise counsel, and friend.

David Van Ness for his deft layouts and calm amid my bookmaking storms.

Lisa Brazieal for keeping the behind-the-scenes production work moving along.

Julie Bess for taking on the indexing work with so little notice—and doing a great job.

Nancy Aldrich-Ruenzel, Peachpit's publisher, for making this work-from-home life possible.

And, as always, Mary.

Finally, my thanks to the friends who so kindly let me use their great photos: Ray Montoya (pages 7, 13, 20), Amy and Kelly Oliver (pages 69–70), and Ken Small (page 112). My heart-felt appreciation also goes to everyone who appears in these photos: the entire Engel clan, Bruce Hammel, Nancy Harbert, Kerry Harder, plus Joshua, Jacob, and Soli. Thanks as well to the beauty of the Colorado Plateau and eastern France.

contents

introduction   vii

what you'll create   viii   the next step   xii
how this book works   x

1. getting ready   1

Welcome screen   2   get from camera   14
File Browser   3   get from scanner   16
Elements Editor   6   get from Organizer   18
arrange work space   7   get from iPhoto   19
set monitor colors   10   reformat photos   20
calibrate monitor   11   extra bits   21
get photos from folders   13

2. make quick fixes   23

rotate photo   24   fix lighting   35
fix flash red eye   26   fix colors   38
crop photo   29   sharpen automatically   40
use smart fix   31   extra bits   42
match the light   34

contents

3. correct exposures   43

undo multiple changes   44
lighten shadows   45
darken highlights   47
adjust midtones   48
read the histogram   49
reduce contrast   52

use levels   54
fix levels with layer   56
fix flashed-out areas   58
add fill flash   60
extra bits   64

4. adjust colors   65

set color management   66
learn color basics   67
adjust with variations   69
fix hue with layer   71
fix skin tone with mask   73

remove color cast   77
remove color noise   78
warm or cool colors   80
convert colors   82
extra bits   84

5. repair & transform photos   85

remove dust, scratches   86
fix blemishes   88
repair areas   89
restore missing areas   92
select part of photo   97

modify selection   100
remove objects   102
combine photos   105
create a panorama   112
extra bits   116

6. share photos   117

print photos   118
email photos   122

save for the web   125
extra bits   129

index   130

introduction

The Visual QuickProject Guide that you hold in your hands offers a unique way to learn about new technologies. Instead of drowning you in theoretical possibilities and lengthy explanations, this Visual QuickProject Guide uses big, color illustrations coupled with clear, concise step-by-step instructions to show you how to complete each photo retouching project in less than an hour.

In this book you'll be retouching your photos using Adobe Photoshop Elements 3, one of the most powerful, yet easy to use image editing programs available. Each chapter walks you through fixing some of the most common—and often bedeviling—problems you'll encounter when working on your photos. By the end of the book, you'll not only know how to deal with these problems, you'll also understand which tools work best in each situation and how to work quickly and efficiently.

Aside from Adobe Photoshop Elements 3, your Windows computer must be running Microsoft Windows XP Professional or Home Edition with Service Pack 1; or Windows 2000 with Service Pack 4. If you're using a Macintosh computer, it should be running at least Mac OS X v.10.2.8 or v.10.3.

You can find this book's companion site at http://www.waywest.net/psevqj/.

You'll find all the example files used in the book, including before and after versions of the photos.

You'll also find extra tips on using Elements, plus general tips about digital photography. Finally, the site includes corrections for any mistakes that might be found after the book was printed.

what you'll create

These two pages represent just some of the photo problems you'll learn how to solve.

Use Elements to quickly fix red eye, a common problem when photographing people with a flash at night or in a darkened room. (See page 26.)

The Auto button, found in the Quick Fix mode, lets you quickly rebalance an over- or under-exposed photo. (See page 35.)

The Standard Edit mode's various tools gives you far more precise control over a photo's shadows and high-lights. (See page 60.)

Easily restore distorted skin tones by adjusting Saturation, Hue, Temperature, and Lightness. (See page 73.)

Rescue torn or faded heirloom photos with some of the advanced tools in Elements. (See page 89.)

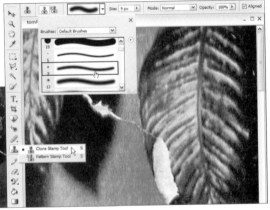

Stitch together a series of side-by-side photos to create wonderfully detailed panoramas that look great as large prints. (See page 112.)

introduction

how this book works

The title explains what is covered in that section.

Names of Elements tools, palettes, and any crucial concepts are shown in orange.

darken highlights

Sometimes you only need to fix the "hotspots" or highlights in a photo. But if you also need to lighten the photo's shadows, do that first as explained in lighten shadows on page 45–46.

1 In Standard Edit mode, open the photo you want to fix and choose Enhance > Adjust Lighting > Shadows/Highlights.

Numbered steps lead you through the sequence of actions, showing only the details you really need.

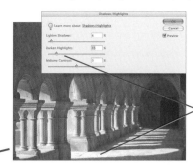

2 When the Shadows/Highlights dialog box opens, the Darken Highlights slider will be at the far left, set at 0. Drag it to the right until the very brightest areas just start to show some detail (in our example, about 15).

Screenshots focus on what part of Elements you'll be using for the particular project step.

3 Be careful not to overcorrect the highlights. In the example, with the slider set to 100, the brightest areas show plenty of detail, but other areas look artificially lit.

We'll finish by adjusting the midtone contrast on the next page.

correct exposures

47

introduction

The extra bits section at the end of each chapter contains additional tips and tricks that you might need to know. Read them in tandem with the particular page you're working on.

use levels

extra bits

The heading for each group of tips matches the section title. (The colors are just for decoration and have no hidden meaning.)

lighten shadows p. 45

- Stay away from using the Enhance > Adjust Lighting > Brightness/Contrast control, because its changes do not distinguish between shadows, highlights, and midtones.

- It's hard to adjust the sliders precisely. Instead, click in the number text window and use the ⊞ or ⊟ keys to change the number a digit at a time. Use [Shift]⊞ or [Shift]⊟ to move in 10-digit steps. The Lighten Shadows and Darken Highlights sliders also appear in the Quick Fix Lighting pane—but without the text windows.

read the histogram p. 49

- To save memory, Elements does not continuously update the histogram. If a yellow triangle appears, click the circular refresh button to update the histogram's display.

use levels p. 54

- Because the histogram's top-to-bottom axis reflects the amount of each value, the balance point will not always fall halfway between the right and left end points.

fix flashed-out area p. 58

- Finding the right levels often takes some trial and error. That's the great thing about adjustment layers: You can change your mind. Just double-click the adjustment layer to re-open its Levels dialog box.

add fill flash p. 60

- This layer-and-brush trick works for fixing a relatively small area in the photo. Need to lighten the entire photo? Click the Normal drop-down menu in the Layers palette and choose Screen. The steps from there are the same as fix flashed-out areas—except that it lightens instead of darkens.

Next to the heading there's a page number that also shows which section the tips belong to.

64   correct exposures

the next step

This Visual QuickProject Guide focuses on fixing common exposure problems, repairing damaged photos, a few cool transformation tricks, and then sharing the results with friends and family. It does not dive deep into all the amazing tools and filters packed into Elements. If you want to learn more about them, try the Photoshop Elements 3 for Windows and Macintosh: Visual QuickStart Guide, by Craig Hoeschen.

CRAIG HOESCHEN

VISUAL QUICKSTART GUIDE

PHOTOSHOP ELEMENTS
FOR WINDOWS & MACINTOSH

Teach yourself Photoshop Elements the quick and easy ' This Visual QuickStart le uses pictures rather than hy explanations. You'll be nd running in no time!

Changing and Adjusting Colors

Lighting Your Image

Overexposed background images and under-exposed foreground subjects are a common problem for most amateur photographers. Photoshop Elements provides an elegant tool to help salvage your otherwise perfect compositions. Much like levels, it operates on pixels in specific tonal ranges (either highlights or shadows) while leaving the other tonal ranges alone. A Lighten Shadows slider helps to add detail to areas in shadow, while a Darken Highlights slider can add detail to washed-out areas in the background.

Figure 3.32 The Shadows/Highlights dialog box.

To improve foreground detail:

1. From the Enhance menu, choose Adjust Lighting > Shadows/Highlights. The Shadows/Highlights dialog box appears (**Figure 3.32**).

2. In the Shadows/Highlights dialog box, drag the Lighten Shadows slider to the right to lessen the effect of the shadows, or to the left to introduce shadow back into the image.

3. Drag the Midtone Contrast slider to the right to increase the contrast, or to the left to decrease the contrast.

4. Click OK to close the Shadows/Highlights dialog box and apply the changes (**Figure 3.33**).

✔ **Tips**

- I've found that in many (if not most) images imported from a digital camera, the Shadows/Highlights dialog box defaults work surprisingly well on their own, requiring just minor slider adjustments.

- In any case, use the Midtone Contrast slider sparingly. A little goes a long way, and adjustments of more than plus or minus 10% can quickly wash out or flatten an image's details.

Figure 3.33 The top photo is a little under-exposed in the foreground, so detail in the young woman's face is hidden in shadow. In the bottom photo, making adjustments with the Lighten Shadows and the Midtone Contrast sliders selectively brightens and enhances detail in both her face and blouse.

LIGHTING YOUR IMAGE

85

The Visual QuickStart Guide teaches you step-by-step how to use every aspect of Elements. Its 400-plus pages are packed with clear examples and helpful tips. Like all the books in Peachpit's Visual QuickStart Guide series, it also works as a reference guide when you just need to learn (or remember) the steps for completing a task.

1. getting ready

Part of what makes taking digital photos so much fun is that you can immediately see if you got the shot. Using Adobe Photoshop Elements, you're about to discover the other part of the digital fun: It's easy to make good shots great. You'll learn how to tweak your photos so that they pop off the screen and page. You'll fix not-quite-perfect shots faster than any darkroom technician. And you'll double your skills to create eye-catching photos to share with your family and friends This chapter's quick overview will get you going. Later chapters will cover all the details you'll need to know.

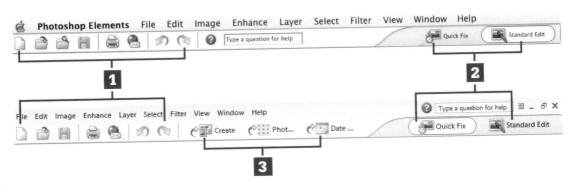

Here is, for example, the shortcuts bar for the Elements editor. Beyond icons for such basic functions as opening, saving, printing, and undoing mistakes **1**, the bar gives you a quick way to switch between Elements' Quick Fix and Standard Edit modes **2**. The Windows shortcuts bar includes buttons for the entirely separate Organizer component **3**, which isn't included in the Mac version.

Welcome screen

When you first launch Elements from your desktop, the Welcome screen appears by default. (See extra bits on page 21.)

In the Windows version of the Welcome screen, you can choose whether to work in the Quick Fix or Standard Edit mode. When the Elements Editor then appears, you find the file you want using the File Browser (⇧Shift Ctrl O) or Open command (Ctrl O). (For more information on the File Browser, see the next page.)

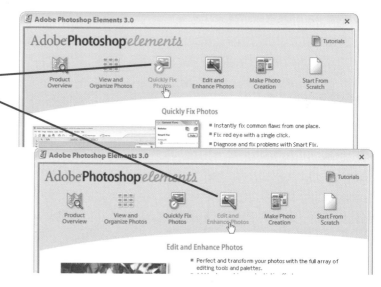

In the Mac version of the Welcome screen, you click the Open File for Editing button, which takes you directly to the File Browser. Any file opened within the File Browser will then appear in Elements' Standard Edit mode.

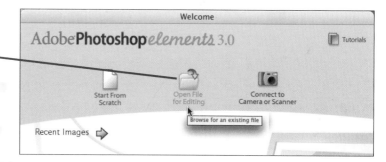

getting ready

File Browser

Initially the File Browser might seem like overkill. But as you hunt down and edit various photos, you'll come to appreciate the browser's ability to jump to specific folders and files. Open the File Browser by pressing ⟨⇧ Shift⟩⟨Ctrl⟩⟨O⟩ in Windows or ⟨⇧ Shift⟩⟨⌘⟩⟨O⟩ on the Mac.

Use the drop-down menu to navigate to a particular folder.

The contents of the folder will appear in the main window.

The Folders pane highlights the selected folder and shows its place in your computer's file directory.

The photo selected in main window appears in this Preview pane, along with information about the photo and data captured by your camera in the Metadata pane.

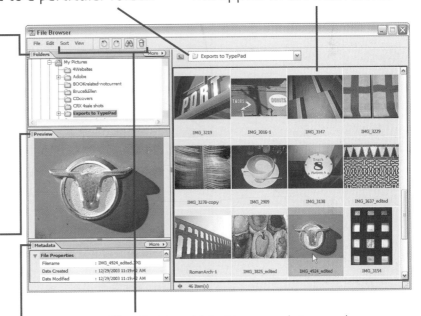

The Sort and View menus let you change the order and size of the main window thumbnails. (See extra bits on page 21.)

Use the circling arrows, binocular, and trash buttons respectively to rotate thumbnails, create searches, and delete photos.

File Browser (cont.)

By rearranging the Folders, Preview, and Metadata panes, you can see more within the individual panes. Click and drag the Preview tab to the top, next to the Folders tab, and then pull down the pane's bottom edge.

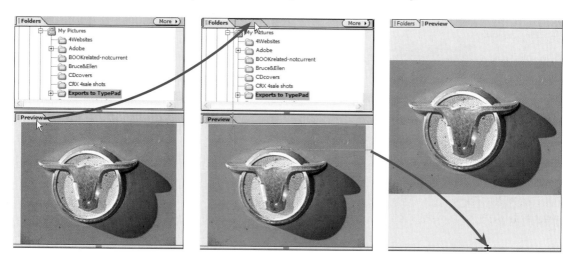

Now when you click the Folders or Metadata tabs, you can see more information without scrolling.

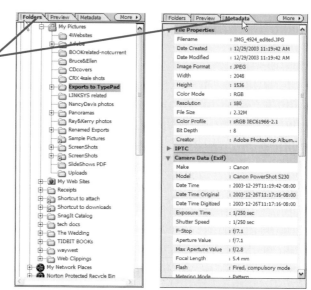

getting ready

To search for a particular folder or photo, click the File Browser's binocular button.

Use the Search dialog box to specify where to look and what to look for, then click Search.

The File Browser's Search Results will display all photos matching your criteria and tell you how many were found at the bottom of the main window.

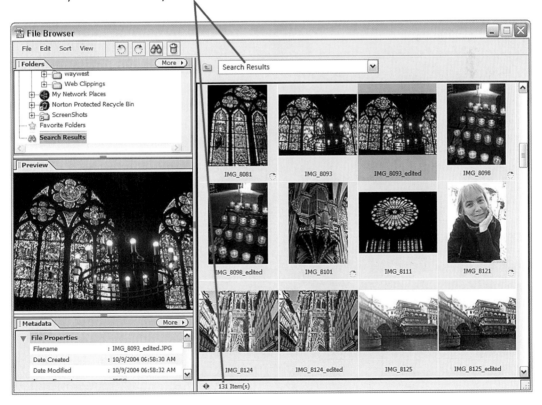

Elements Editor

The Elements Editor offers two modes: Quick Fix and Standard Edit. Quick Fix lets you make simple corrections for the most common photo problems. When you need more control—fine-tuning a particular aspect or changing a selected part of the photo—use Standard Edit.

In both edit modes, the Toolbox runs down the left side of the main window with the related Options Bar across the top of the window. Your choices in the Options Bar change depending on which tool you select.

By clicking either tab, you can jump between Quick Fix and Standard Edit.

In Quick Fix, the Palette Bin offers a few simple sliders to fix photos; the Standard Edit palette is packed with controls for more complex fixes. The Quick Fix palette is locked in place, but you can reposition every pane in the Standard Edit palette. (See arrange work space on the next page.)

The Photo Bin displays thumbnails of every photo open at the moment, and puts a blue border around the photo being displayed in the main window. Click another thumbnail to see that photo in the main window.

getting ready

arrange work space

Digital cameras make it so easy to take lots of photos, you'll find yourself using Elements a lot. Make yourself at home—and work more efficiently—by arranging the editing workspace just as you like it. If you're using a laptop with a small screen, you'll find it very helpful to collapse the Palette and Photo bins.

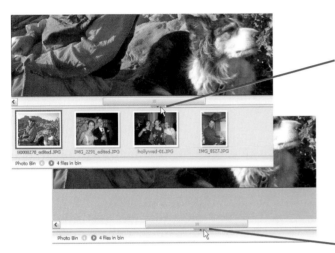

In either editing mode, you can gain some screen real estate by collapsing the Photo Bin. In Windows, single-click (double-click on the Mac) the thin arrow-bar separating the main window from the Photo Bin below. Then, expand your photo to fill the larger main window by choosing Ctrl O (Windows) or ⌘ O (Mac). To expand the Palette Bin back to its full size, single- or double-click the bar again.

Here's another way to collapse or expand the Photo Bin: In Windows, single-click the green arrow at the bin's bottom left or on the Mac, click the round green button at the bin's upper left.

To restore the bin to its full size, just single-click the arrow or button again. Remember to expand your photo to fill the larger main window using Ctrl O (Windows) or ⌘ O (Mac).

arrange work space (cont.)

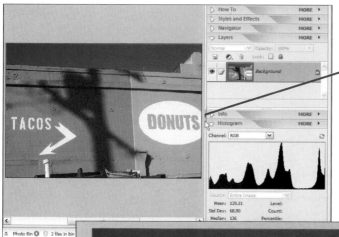

Collapsing the Palette Bin creates lots of elbow room. As with the Photo Bin, single-click (Windows) or double-click (Mac) the thin arrow-bar separating the main window from the bin on the right.

Use Ctrl O (Windows) or ⌘ O (Mac) to expand your photo to fill the expanded main window. Repeat to restore the Palette Bin. (See extra bits on page 21.)

If you only need one or two palettes for the moment, why let the Palette Bin hog your screen? Instead, click the needed palette's top tab, and drag it to a new spot on top of the photo.

Now, collapse the Palette Bin as explained on page 8, and drag it to a new spot.

Then, expand your photo to take advantage of the extra space, using Ctrl O (Windows) or ⌘ O (Mac).

Finally, you can hide or reveal the details of any Palette pane by single-clicking its tab.

set monitor colors

Most likely your monitor is already set to display colors at its highest quality. But let's make sure.

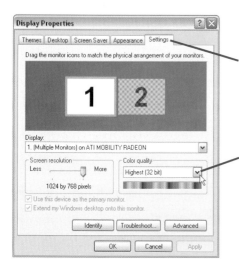

For Windows, choose Start > Control Panel > Display and click the Settings tab.

Make sure the Color quality panel is set to Highest (32 bit) or True Color (24 bit) and click OK to close.

On a Mac, click the menu bar's Apple menu, choose System Preferences, and then choose Display at the top of the dialog box that appears. By default, the Display pane will appear.

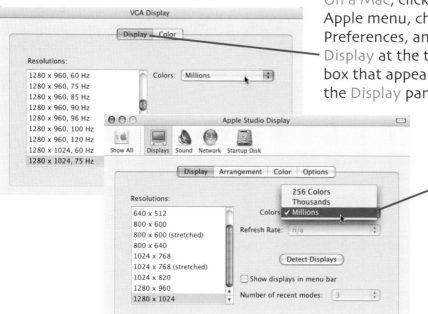

Check the Colors pop-up menu to make sure it's set to Millions or Thousands, then press ⌘Q to close the dialog box.

calibrate monitor

Calibration is only possible if you're using a traditional monitor with a cathode ray tube (CRT). It's not practical for an LCD monitor (all laptops or any thin-flat external monitor) because the LCD's apparent brightness changes with your angle of view. (See extra bits on page 21 for a workaround.)

Windows users should choose Start > Control Panel > Adobe Gamma.

If Adobe Gamma is not a choice, do this instead: navigate here on your C hard drive (that's your main drive): ~\C:\Program Files\Common Files\ Adobe\Calibration\ and double-click Adobe Gamma.

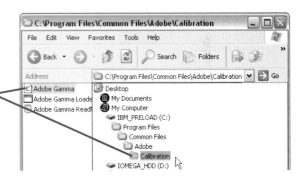

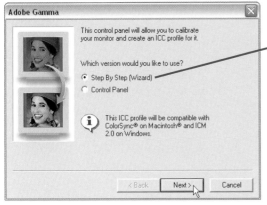

When the Adobe Gamma dialog box appears, choose Step By Step (Wizard), click Next, and follow the instructions.

calibrate monitor (cont.)

Mac users should click the menu bar's Apple menu, choose System Preferences, and then choose Display at the top of the dialog box that appears.

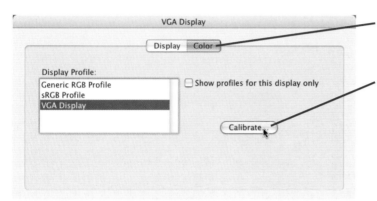

Select the Color button in the VGA Display dialog box and then click Calibrate.

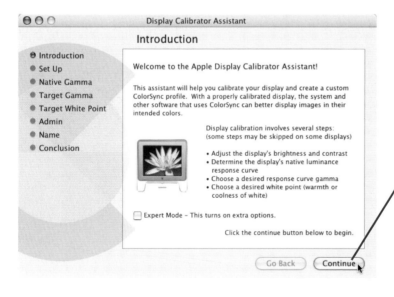

When the Display Calibrator Assistant appears, choose Continue, and follow the instructions. When you're done, click Close, and then press ⌘Q to close the VGA Display dialog box.

get photos from folders

Not surprisingly, the File Browser offers the easiest way to find photos in your folders and open them for editing.

1 Open the File Browser ([Ctrl][O] in Windows, [⌘][O] on the Mac).

2 Navigate to the folder holding the photo you want to change.

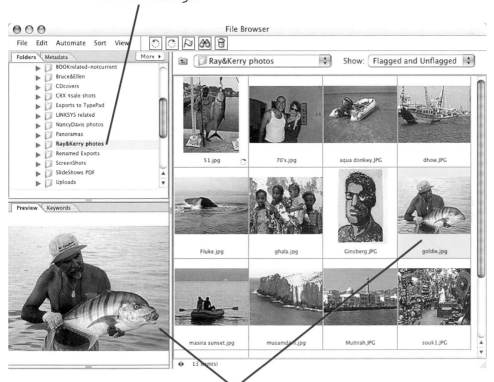

3 Once you find the thumbnail image of the photo you want to edit, double-click it in either the main window or Preview pane to open it.

get from camera

Because the Windows and Mac versions of Elements differ, the process for getting photos from your camera or card reader is just a bit different.

1 In the Mac version of Elements, make sure your camera or loaded card-reader is connected. (If iPhoto tries to launch automatically and take over the process, press ⌘Q.)

2 Launch Elements and choose File > Open to navigate to the camera or card reader, which will appear in the left sidebar.

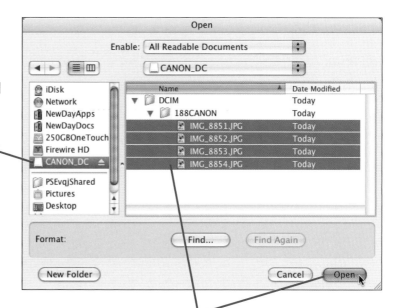

3 Once you find the folder you need, choose the images you want to edit in Elements. The photos will open in the Elements Editor, ready for retouching. Before continuing, save the images onto your computer. (See reformat photos on page 20.)

1 In the Windows version of Elements, make sure your camera or loaded card-reader is connected. (If the Adobe Photo Downloader tries to take over the process, see the extra bits on page 22.)

2 Switch from Elements' Editor to its Organizer by clicking the Photo Browser button in the Shortcuts bar. When the Organizer appears, click the camera button in the Shortcuts bar and choose From Camera or Card Reader in the drop-down menu.

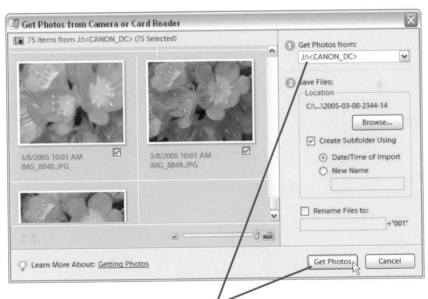

3 Select your camera or card in the Get Photos from drop-down menu and click Get Photos. The photos will be copied to your computer and appear in the Organizer, where you can open them for retouching in the Editor. (See the second step in get from Organizer on page 18.)

get from scanner

No doubt you have photos not shot with a digital camera that you'd like to fix. A scanner makes it simple to move prints onto your computer. If you've already used a program included with the scanner to import photos, then just follow the steps in get photos from folders on page 13. If you want to import scanner images directly into Elements, the process is slightly different for Macs and Windows.

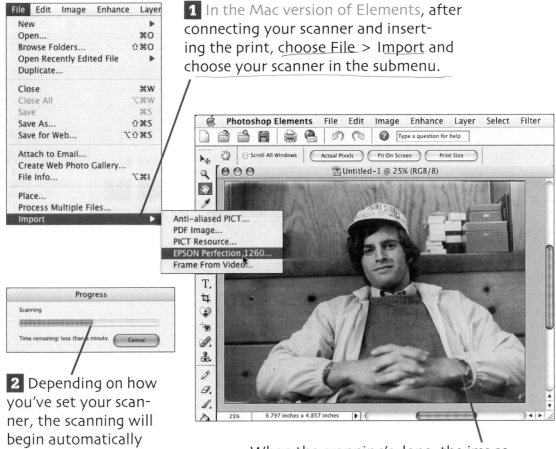

1 In the Mac version of Elements, after connecting your scanner and inserting the print, choose File > Import and choose your scanner in the submenu.

2 Depending on how you've set your scanner, the scanning will begin automatically or you may need to start it manually. A progress bar will track the scanning.

When the scanning's done, the image will appear in Elements' Editor. Before continuing, save the images onto your computer.

1 In the Windows version of Elements, switch from Elements' Editor to its Organizer by clicking the Photo Browser button in the Shortcuts bar.

2 When the Organizer appears, click the camera button in the Shortcuts bar and choose From Scanner in the drop-down menu. A progress bar will track the scanning. When it's done, the photos will appear in the Organizer, where you can open them for retouching in the Editor. (See the second step in get from Organizer on the next page.)

get from Organizer

If you're using the Windows version of Elements, the Organizer makes it easy to find photos and then fix them within the Editor. (Mac users: see get from iPhoto on the next page.)

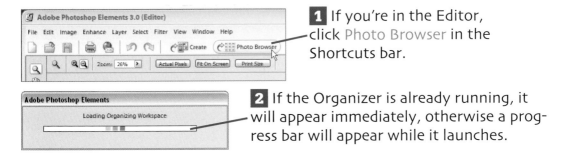

1 If you're in the Editor, click Photo Browser in the Shortcuts bar.

2 If the Organizer is already running, it will appear immediately, otherwise a progress bar will appear while it launches.

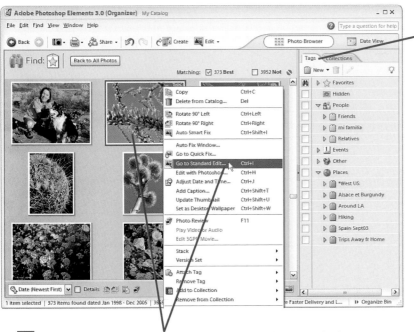

3 You can then use your Tags, or any of the Organizer's many sort tools, to find the photo you want to fix.

4 Once you find the photo, right-click it and choose either Go to Quick Fix or Go to Standard Edit from the drop-down menu. The photo will then appear back in Elements' Editor for retouching.

get from iPhoto

If you're on a Mac and prefer to use iPhoto for importing or organizing your photos, you can still edit them using Elements' more powerful Editor.

1 Launch iPhoto and from the menu bar, choose iPhoto > Preferences. In the General pane, select Opens photos in. The Open dialog box appears automatically.

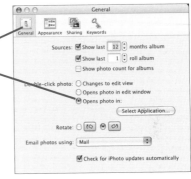

2 Use the dialog box to navigate to where you've installed Elements and click Open. When the Preferences dialog box reappears, close it by clicking the red button in the upper left.

3 Now you can double-click a photo within iPhoto and it will auto-matically open in Elements' Editor. Make your fixes, save the photo in Elements, close it, and the photo will be updated in iPhoto.

reformat photos

Most digital cameras save photos as JPEG (or JPG) files because they're compact yet capture lots of detail. Unfortunately, every time you resave a JPG file, which you'll do as you edit and re-edit, it throws away data. By saving your newly imported photos as TIFF files, you can retouch without losing crucial detail. Later, if you want to send out an email or Web version, Elements can automatically convert the TIFF. (See extra bits on page 22; share photos on page 117.)

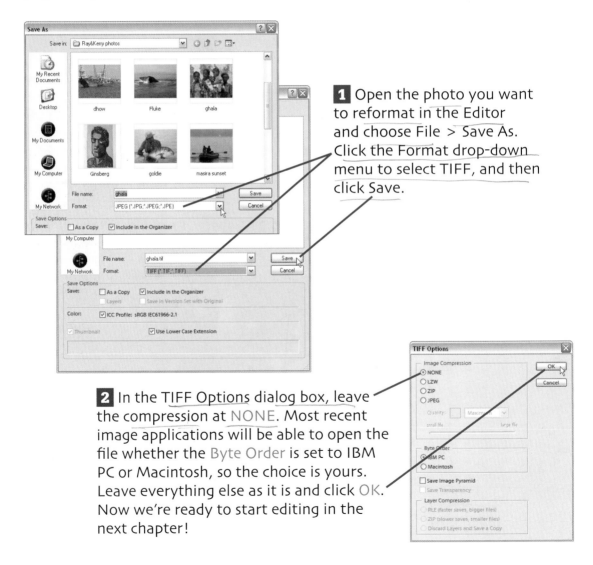

1 Open the photo you want to reformat in the Editor and choose File > Save As. Click the Format drop-down menu to select TIFF, and then click Save.

2 In the TIFF Options dialog box, leave the compression at NONE. Most recent image applications will be able to open the file whether the Byte Order is set to IBM PC or Macintosh, so the choice is yours. Leave everything else as it is and click OK. Now we're ready to start editing in the next chapter!

extra bits

Welcome screen p. 2

- If you want to bypass the Welcome screen and start up directly in the Editor view, click the drop-down menu in the bottom-left and select Editor (Windows) or, on the Mac, uncheck the Show at Startup box, also at the bottom-left of the Welcome screen.

File Browser p. 3

- The Sort menu includes Custom, which lets you click-and-drag thumbnails within the File Browser to arrange them exactly as you want. The View menu includes Details, which will display basic information for every photo in the File Browser's main window.

arrange work space p. 8

- The Windows Palette Bin also can be collapsed or expanded by clicking on the green arrow at the bottom of the bin.

calibrate monitor p. 11

- Many monitors now are self-calibrating, which makes this step unnecessary. Check your display's manual to make sure.
- If you're using an LCD monitor, open a photo file that has an even range of colors and tones, from bright to dark. Adjust the LCD's angle to minimize any glare or distortion in the image. (In contrast, if you crank the LCD nearly flat you'll see how it distorts the color of the image.) Similarly, work away from bright sun or windows when you're retouching your photos, since that will skew your perception of the image.
- If you're lucky enough to have a CRT and LCD monitor, run Elements's Editor on the CRT screen for the best results.

extra bits

get from camera p. 14

- Windows users getting photos may have to battle the Adobe Photo Downloader, which auto-launches whenever you connect a camera or load a flash card. For me, it adds an unwanted step. To disable it, open the Organizer preferences (Edit > Preferences > Camera or Card Reader) and uncheck Use Adobe Photo Downloader....

- When Elements offers to erase your card after importing photos, click No to avoid accidentally erasing any photos. Reformat the card with your camera, not the computer.

reformat photos p. 20

- If you're lucky enough to have a newer, high-end digital camera that saves photos in the RAW format, stay with that since it's even better than using TIFF files.

- Windows users should check Include in the Organizer. The photo will be stored with all the other versions of the photo, no matter what their format.

- Yes, it's tempting, but resist renaming all your images from their arbitrary numbers to something you'll recognize. The whole point of date-and-keyword programs like the Organizer (or iPhoto) is to make it easy to find your photos, no matter what they're named.

getting ready

2. make quick fixes

The Quick Fix mode helps you correct the most common—and easiest to solve—problems found in photos. Like the Quick Fix pane itself, this chapter starts with general items like rotating and red-eye, then makes lighting and color adjustments, and ends with sharpening. Always work in that order. If you apply sharpening first, for example, your results will not look as good.

① Rotate ② red-eye
③ light + color adjustments
④ sharpening

Before any fixes, the top-left photo suffers from the usual problems: red-eye, too-dark shadows, overly bright highlights, and a slight color cast.

The lower-right version shows the fixes explained in this chapter. And the fixes really are quick: it only took two minutes to apply them all.

rotate photo

Digital cameras have become so good at sensing when you're shooting a vertical image that you rarely need to manually rotate photos. Still, there's always the exception. Photos can be rotated in Quick Fix mode or Standard Edit mode, though the buttons are available only in Quick Fix. (See extra bits on page 42.)

1 Make sure you're working in Quick Fix mode, then open the File Browser (⇧Shift Ctrl O in Windows, ⇧Shift ⌘ O on the Mac).

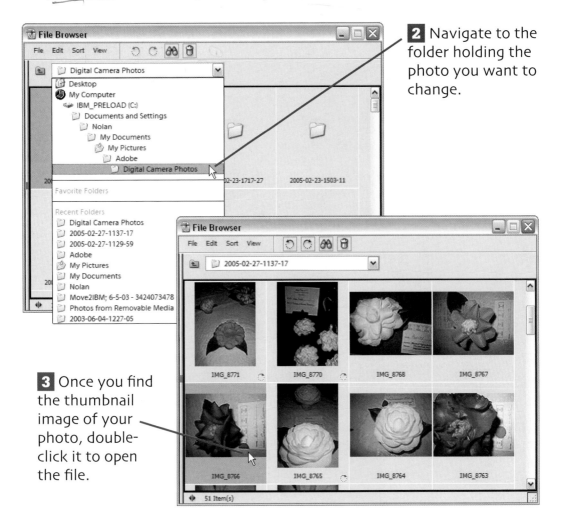

2 Navigate to the folder holding the photo you want to change.

3 Once you find the thumbnail image of your photo, double-click it to open the file.

make quick fixes

4 Click the rotate left or right button in the General Fixes section of the Palette Bin.

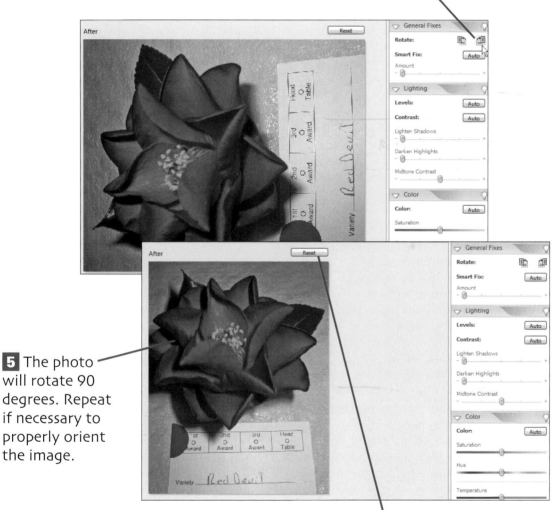

5 The photo will rotate 90 degrees. Repeat if necessary to properly orient the image.

6 If you change your mind, click Reset and the image will return to its original orientation.

fix flash red eye

Take a flash shot of people in a darkened room and almost inevitably the centers of their eyes will appear blood red. Fortunately, this is easy to fix. The red eye tool and technique work the same whether you're in Quick Fix mode or Standard Edit mode. (See extra bits on page 42.)

2 Select the Zoom tool in the Toolbox.

1 Open the photo you want to fix and set the drop-down menu in the main window to Before and After (Portrait).

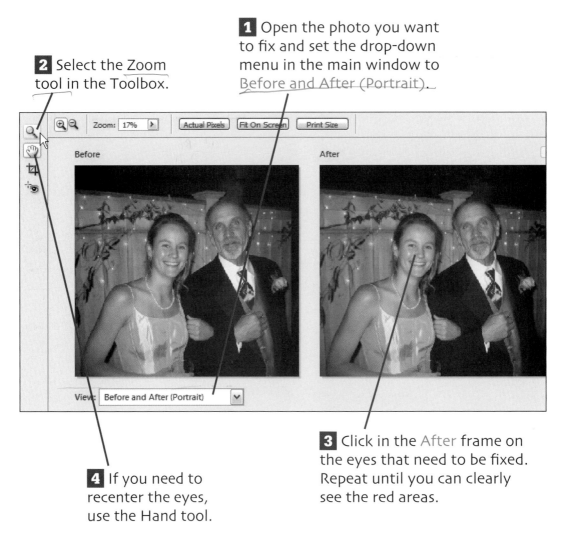

4 If you need to recenter the eyes, use the Hand tool.

3 Click in the After frame on the eyes that need to be fixed. Repeat until you can clearly see the red areas.

make quick fixes

5 Click the Toolbox's Red Eye Removal tool.

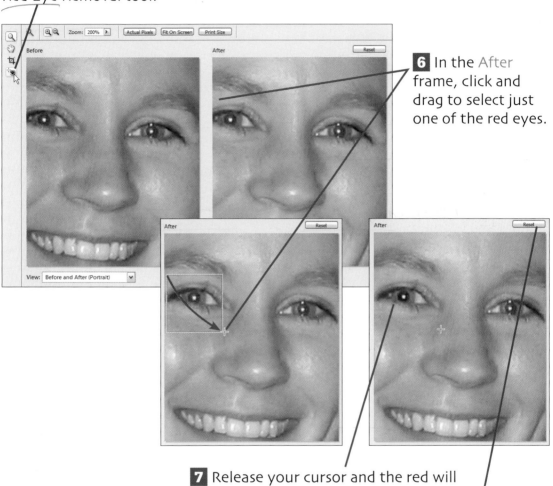

6 In the After frame, click and drag to select just one of the red eyes.

7 Release your cursor and the red will be removed. Repeat the same steps to remove red from the other eye.

8 If you're not happy with the results, click Reset and see the next step.

make quick fixes

fix flash red eye (cont.)

9 The red eye tool sometimes needs a little help finding and removing all the red. By default, the red eye tool is set at 50-50 in the Options Bar, so it darkens exactly half of the pupil's size by half its original darkness (the photo equivalent of an F-stop).

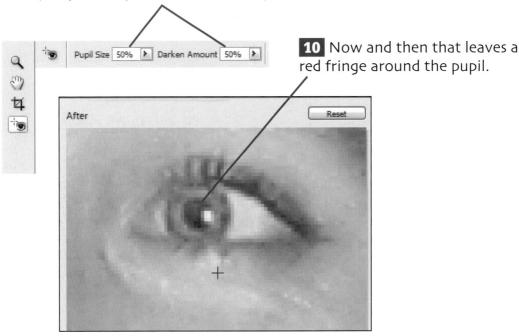

10 Now and then that leaves a red fringe around the pupil.

11 To fix it, click the Pupil Size drop-down menu in the tool's Options Bar and move the slider a little to the right.

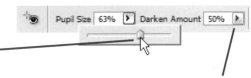

12 If you find the tool is turning red eyes pinkish-gray instead of black, drag the Darken Amount slider to the right.

13 When you're done reapplying the red eye fix, reset the tool, and it will return to the 50-50 default.

crop photo

Make a rough crop of your photos before you dive into fixing any exposure or color problems. After you've fixed everything else, you can then come back and make a second, final crop to put the borders exactly where you want them. (See extra bits on page 42.)

Open the photo you want to crop in either Quick Fix mode or Standard Edit mode.

The Crop Tool works the same in either mode, though its location in the Toolbox changes.

If you're in Quick Fix mode, use the View drop-down menu to switch to any view other than Before Only, which won't let you crop.

crop photo (cont.)

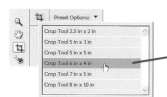

If you'll eventually want prints of the photo, choose a crop ratio from the Preset Options drop-down menu. In the example, we've chosen 6 in x 4 in since that's the most popular print size.

1 Click and drag in the main window, where your preset ratio will be used as you position the crop box.

2 Release the cursor and, if necessary, click the Hand Tool if you need to reposition the overall position of the crop. (To switch back, click the Crop Tool again.)

3 To resize a particular side, click and drag any corner of the crop box.

5 If you don't like the results, click Reset.

4 To apply the crop, double-click the photo or click the check mark.

use smart fix

Smart Fix essentially lets you retouch a photo with a single click. If you don't like the effect, which applies a combination of lighting and color fixes, you can adjust the amount with the slider. If you need more control, see the fix lighting and fix color sections on pages 35–39. (See extra bits on page 42.)

1 Open the photo you want to fix in Quick Fix mode and set the main window's drop-down menu to Before and After (Portrait or Landscape). Choose the one that best shows the main part of your photo, repositioning if necessary with the Hand and Zoom tools.

Quick Fix – set main window to Before and after

2 If the General Fixes pane isn't already showing in the Palette Bin, click its triangle.

use smart fix (cont.)

3 Click Auto to apply the Smart Fix.

4 In the example, Smart Fix lightened the black dress a tad too much, making it look gray. We'll click Reset to cancel the effect.

make quick fixes

5 Drag the Amount slider to find the best balance between lightening the dark areas without washing out the light areas.

6 Once you find the right spot for the slider, click the ✔ to apply the effect or press ⌐←Enter⌐ (Windows) or ⌐Return⌐ (Mac).

match the light

Here's a quick bit of background before using the Quick Fix Lighting pane, which controls levels and contrast, two key aspects of your photo's exposure. Levels refer to a photo's overall mix of tones, from light (highlights) to midtones to dark (shadows). Contrast refers to the amount of difference between a photo's lightest and darkest tones.

In the stork photo on the left, there's so little contrast that it's all gray midtones with virtually no highlights or shadows.

The street-scene photo on the right has great contrast, but a skewed mix of lighting levels. Its shadows are too dark to show any detail, while the sun reflecting off the windows is so bright that the highlights are completely washed out.

In general, you want the mix of levels to match the light you saw when you took the shot. That mix, of course, varies from scene to scene. Night scenes naturally have more shadows, mid-day desert scenes more highlights. The Lighting pane cannot work miracles by resurrecting badly exposed photos like these two. But if you start with a halfway decent exposure, the Lighting pane can take your photo the rest of the way.

fix lighting

When using the Quick Fix Lighting pane, the Levels Auto button will adjust a photo's levels and color. The Contrast Auto button affects only the contrast and leaves the colors unchanged. Feel free to experiment: The difference can be subtle or dramatic, depending on your photo. But if you're happy with the colors, use Contrast Auto, as in the example below.

1 Open the photo you want to fix in Quick Fix mode and set the main window's drop-down menu to Before and After (Portrait or Landscape). Choose the one that best shows the main part of your photo, repositioning if necessary with the Hand and Zoom tools.

2 If the Lighting pane isn't already showing in the Palette Bin, click its triangle.

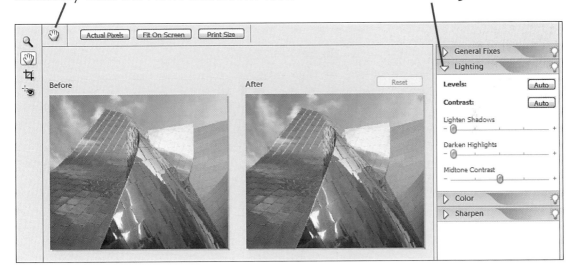

fix lighting (cont.)

3 Click Auto to
fix the contrast.

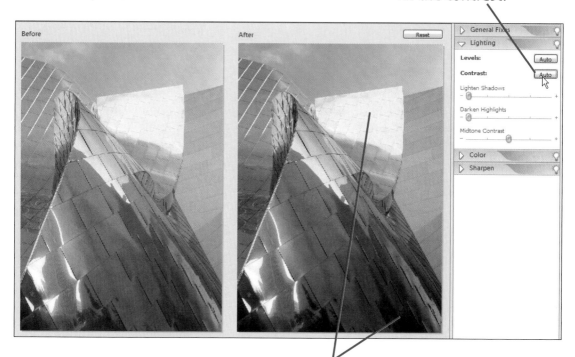

4 In the example, the Quick Fix does
a pretty good job at reducing the
glare off Disney Hall's stainless steel
while preserving shadow details. But
we can do better.

make quick fixes

5 By first dragging the Darken Highlights slider a tiny bit to the right, we take out the last bit of glare.

6 Now Lighten Shadows a bit by dragging that slider to the right. (In both cases, dragging to the right increases the effect; to the left reduces it.)

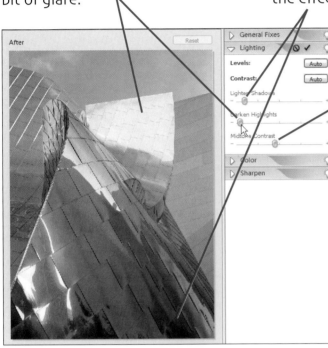

7 By moving the Middle Contrast slider ever so slightly to the left, the steel's midtones lose any harshness. (This slider normally sits at the middle tick mark.)

8 That's much better than the original image, so apply the change by clicking the ✔ or pressing ←Enter (Windows) or Return (Mac).

fix colors

You'll find that the Quick Fix Color pane's Auto button does a fairly good job of adjusting skin tones so they look more natural. It does this by applying a neutral color cast to the photo's midtones, plus white and black areas.

1 Open the photo you want to fix in Quick Fix mode and set the main window's drop-down menu to Before and After (Portrait or Landscape). Choose the one that best shows the main part of your photo, repositioning if necessary with the Hand and Zoom tools.

2 If the Color pane isn't already showing in the Palette Bin, click its triangle.

3 Click Auto to fix the color.

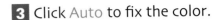

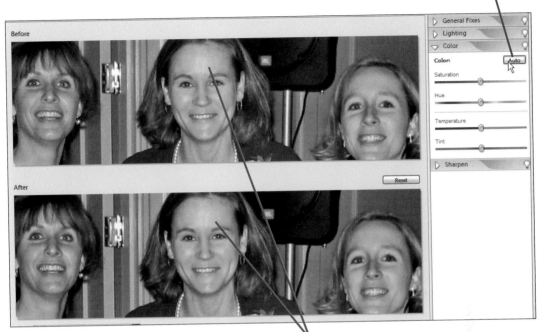

4 As you can see in the example, the effect can be very subtle, almost a matter of taste. In the Before pane, the skin tones have a slight green cast, which has been removed in the After pane.

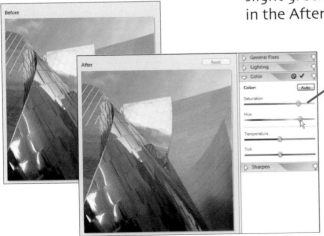

5 While the Color pane includes four sliders, they are so sensitive that you really can't use them for subtle adjustments of things like skin tones. But they can be fun for creating surreal colors in non-people photos. For finer control over colors, see adjust colors on page 65.

sharpen automatically

It's common for digital photos to lose a bit of sharpness as you work on them. The Sharpen pane helps fix that by increasing the contrast along the edges of objects. But be careful. Too much sharpening will make the photo look fake, as if the foreground objects are pasted onto the background.

1 Open the photo you want to sharpen in Quick Fix mode and set the main window's drop-down menu to Before and After (Portrait or Landscape). Avoid zooming in very much because you won't be able to accurately judge the sharpening's effect.

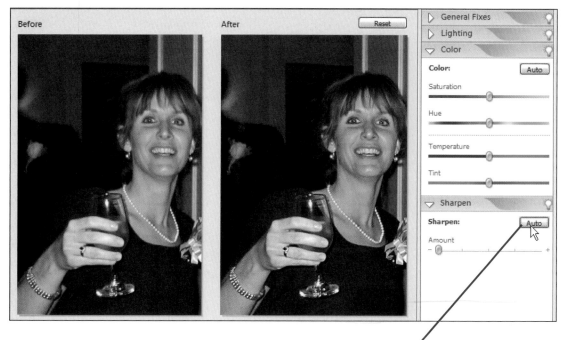

2 Click Auto to apply the sharpening. The effect should be subtle, adding just a bit of crispness.

make quick fixes

3 You can zoom in to see the effect at the pixel-by-pixel level.

4 By dragging the slider all the way to the right, you can clearly see the speckly distortion created by over sharpening.

5 To cancel, click Reset or the ⊘.

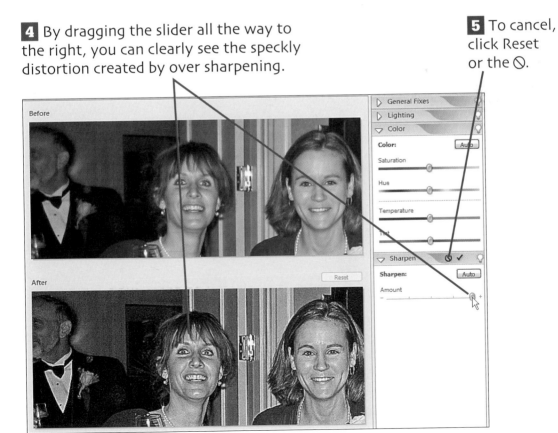

extra bits

rotate photo p. 24

- To rotate images within Standard Edit mode, choose Image > Rotate and make a choice from the drop-down menu.

- Beyond the standard 90° and 180° button choices, you also can rotate a photo by just a few degrees—extremely handy if the horizon in your landscape shot is a bit crooked. From Quick Fix or Standard Edit modes, choose Image > Rotate > Custom and when the Rotate Canvas dialog box appears, enter a number in the Angle window and click OK.

- If you're using the Windows version of Elements, remember the File Browser is not the same thing as the Photo Browser. You can reach the File Browser from either Quick Fix mode or Standard Edit mode, while the Photo Browser is only available within Elements' Organizer.

fix flash red eye p. 26

- More and more digital cameras now have a red-eye reduction flash, which uses a blinking light to shrink the subject's pupil before firing the main flash. You also can reduce red eye by taking pictures at a slight angle to your subject's eyes.

- The red eye tool does not work as consistently if you select both eyes together.

crop photo p. 29

- If possible, it's best to crop your image before shooting by moving closer to your subject. The more you crop after you take the picture, the harder it becomes to produce a big print that's still sharp because, in effect, you're throwing away pixels.

- To cancel the crop before you apply it, click the Options Bar's ⊘ or press [Esc].

use smart fix p. 31

- While you could use Smart Fix in Standard Edit mode by choosing Enhance from the menu bar, using Quick Fix mode is better since you can compare Before and After views, as well as use the slider adjustment.

- Don't zoom in so close on your Before and After views that you can't see the overall effect of the Smart Fix.

- Clicking Auto repeatedly will only muddy the photo; hit Reset and start fresh.

Do Not overclick
Start fresh

3. correct exposures

The Standard Edit mode offers far more control than the Quick Fix mode for correcting a photo's exposure problems. By combining the Element's Levels dialog box, adjustment layers, and a few items from the Toolbox, you can fix even the most challenging exposures.

undo multiple changes

When working in Quick Fix mode, the standard undo command (Ctrl Z in Windows, ⌘ Z on the Mac) is all you need. But as you edit your photos in Standard Edit mode you'll quickly learn to appreciate the Undo History palette. As long as you haven't yet saved your edits, the palette lets you step back through all your changes. That frees you to plunge into photo editing's necessary trial-and-error process without fear. (See extra bits on page 64.)

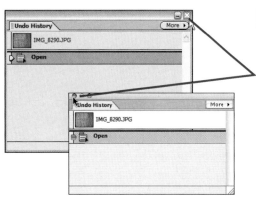

1 In the menu bar, choose Window > Undo History and the Undo History palette will appear in the Palette Bin. If it appears instead as a free-floating palette, click the red button (in the upper right in Windows, upper left on the Mac) and it will close and reappear within the Palette Bin.

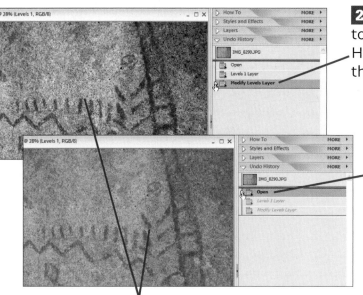

2 As you make changes to the photo, the Undo History palette tracks the steps.

3 To undo a step or multiple steps, click and drag the palette marker.

4 The photo will immediately reflect the undo—this is useful for comparing the before and after states of a multi-step fix.

lighten shadows

This technique works best in Standard Edit mode, where it's easier to control. We'll start here with the shadows, then fix the highlights on the next page, and if necessary, finish by tweaking the midtone contrast on page 48. (See extra bits on page 64.)

1 In our example, many details are obscured in the shadows, while a few of the brightest areas are blasted out.

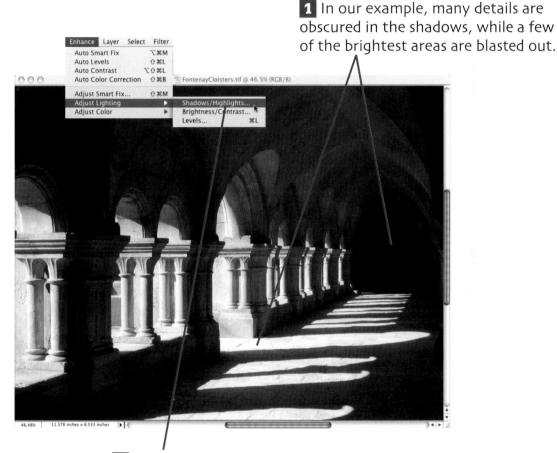

2 In Standard Edit mode, open the photo you want to fix and choose Enhance > Adjust Lighting > Shadows/Highlights.

lighten shadows (cont.)

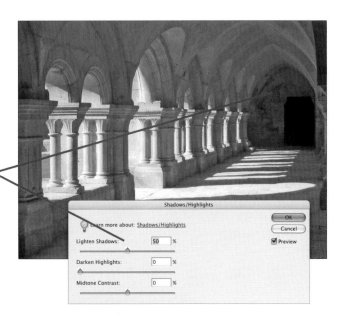

3 When the Shadows/ Highlights dialog box opens, it immediately lightens the shadows by the default value of 50 percent. That's way too much for this example.

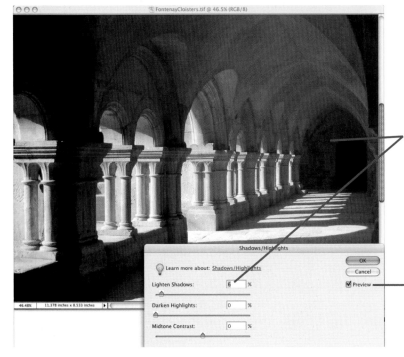

4 Move the Lighten Shadows slider left to 6, which in this case, opens up the shadows without wiping out the dramatic lighting.

5 Use the Preview checkbox to gauge what looks best. Next, we'll fix those hightlights.

correct exposures

darken highlights

Sometimes you only need to fix the "hotspots" or highlights in a photo. But if you also need to lighten the photo's shadows, do that first as explained in lighten shadows on pages 45–46.

1 In Standard Edit mode, open the photo you want to fix and choose Enhance > Adjust Lighting > Shadows/Highlights.

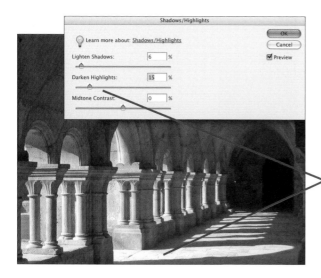

2 When the Shadows/Highlights dialog box opens, the Darken Highlights slider will be at the far left, set at 0. Drag it to the right until the very brightest areas just start to show some detail (in our example, about 15).

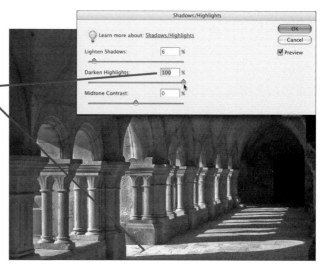

3 Be careful not to overcorrect the highlights. In the example, with the slider set to 100, the brightest areas show plenty of detail, but other areas look artificially lit.

We'll finish by adjusting the midtone contrast on the next page.

adjust midtones

Even when your photo has a good range of shadows and highlights, it may need a bit more "pop." You can get exactly that by adjusting the brightness of the midtones—without affecting the shadows or highlights.

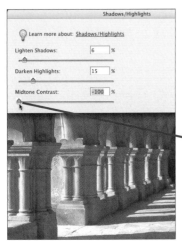

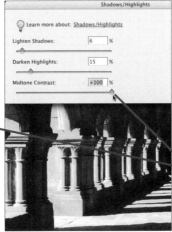

Adjusting the midtone contrast too far in either direction can wreck all your previous fixes in the shadows and highlights.

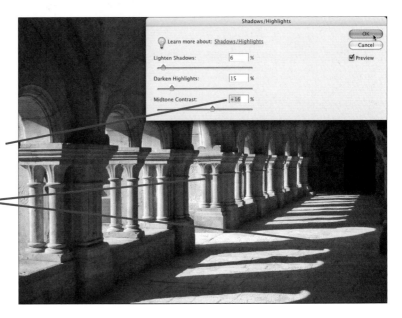

In our example, we've increased the midtone contrast to +16, which preserves the naturalness of the scene in both the darker and lighter midtones.

Save your fixes and you're done.

read the histogram

As we saw on the previous pages, you can make most basic exposure adjustments with just the Shadows/Highlights dialog box. But if you learn how to read Elements' histogram, you'll have a better sense of what's wrong with a problem exposure—and how to fix it. Open the histogram by choosing Window > Histogram and it will appear in the Palette Bin. It might look a bit strange, but it's actually pretty easy to understand. Take a look at the histograms for the next four photos. (See extra bits on page 64.)

From left to right, the histogram shows the range of tones from pure black to pure white.

The top-to-bottom axis shows how much of each tone the photo contains.

This shot of a Utah canyon has few shadows, so it's not surprising that the histogram is weighted toward the right (brighter) side. But notice how the histogram stops short of reaching the far-left side. That means the photo lacks any pure black. On page 56, we'll slightly boost the contrast to improve its tonal range.

correct exposures

read the histogram (cont.)

Dominated by shadows, the histogram for this photo of a French cloister is almost the opposite of the canyon's.

At the far right, you do see a spike of almost pure white, representing the sky.

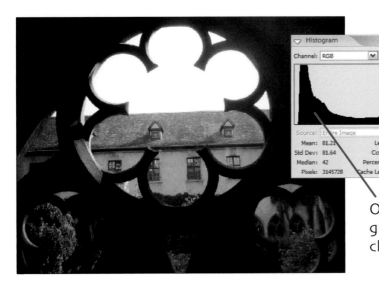

Overall, however, the histogram is skewed to the left, clipping off the black.

As the histogram shows, the photo of the two storks has a full range of tones from pure black to pure white.

On page 52, however, we'll rebalance it by reducing the contrast.

The flower histogram shows an almost ideal exposure: an evenly spread, full range of tones.

Now that you can read the histogram, let's use it to fix the stork photo.

reduce contrast

The stork photo on page 50 suffers from too much contrast, with all blacks or whites and few midtones. By watching the histogram as we use the Shadows/Highlights dialog box, we can accurately reduce the contrast.

1 Open the photo you want to fix in Standard Edit mode and make sure the histogram is visible (Window > Histogram). Choose Enhance > Adjust Lighting > Shadows/Highlights.

2 When the Shadows/Highlights dialog box opens, it automatically lightens the shadows by 50 percent.

3 The histogram's gray areas show how the photo's darkest areas were bunched up on the left before the Lighten Shadows adjustment.

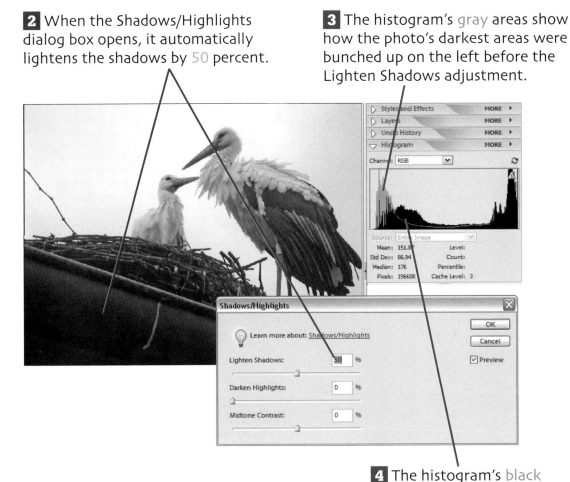

4 The histogram's black areas show the new settings.

5 Because the shadows were lightened a little too much, we'll reduce the setting from 50 to 35 percent, based on some trial and error. We'll also darken the highlights by 9 percent. Most importantly, we'll reduce the Midtone Contrast by 13 percent (−13).

6 The histogram shows that the lightest areas have shifted toward the middle, and the midtones have also increased, compared to the light line marking their original levels.

7 The entire photo is less contrasty, especially in the sky and feathers.

8 While you could make these adjustments by eyeball, the histogram provides feedback that you're on the right track. Save your changes before closing the photo.

use levels

Sometimes, you may need a bit more control than the Shadows/Highlights commands can offer. That's the time to use Elements' Levels command. Take a look at the Levels dialog box for any photo by pressing Ctrl L (Windows) or ⌘ L (Mac). The changes in the example photos below are far greater than normal, just to clearly show their effects.

The Levels dialog box has its own histogram, plus sliders and text fields for adjusting a photo's brightness levels.

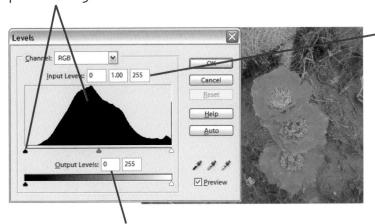

Before any adjustments are made, the Input Levels are set to 0, 1.00, and 255, which represent respectively the brightness/contrast levels for the shadows, midtones, and highlights.

In general, the Output Levels are seldom used to control exposure.

The sliders for the Input Levels control the range of tones (or contrast) in the photo by setting the values for the darkest shadows (the black point) and lightest hightlights (the white point). The respective text fields can do the same with more precision.

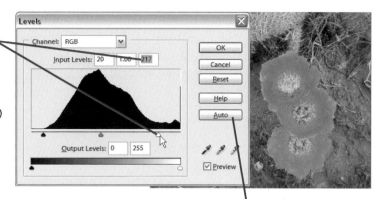

As in Quick Fix mode, the Auto button offers a one-click-to-fix option.

The Input Levels' middle slider (and text field) control the brightness of the photo's midtones— without affecting the shadows or highlights.

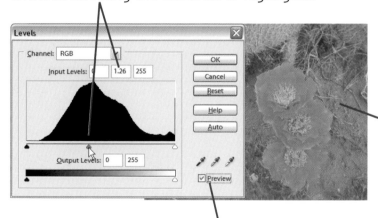

The Preview button lets you compare before and after views of the changes.

Think of the middle slider (the gray one) as the base of a see-saw: Ideally, you position it so that half the histogram's volume sits to the left (the shadows) and half to the right (the highlights). Compare this photo to the one on page 54, and you'll see that the shadow area remains the same while the midtones are brighter.

correct exposures

fix levels with layer

While you can adjust the levels directly, it's much better to do it with an adjustment layer. That's because it lets you change the levels at any time without permanently tossing away any exposure information. If you change the levels directly, the changes are locked in and cannot be tweaked later. Let's see how adjusting the levels can improve the canyon photo on page 49. We'll start by boosting the contrast since the histogram shows few true blacks.

1 In Standard Edit mode, open the photo you want to fix and make sure the Histogram and Layers palettes appear in the Palette Bin (Window > Layers). Click the Adjustment Layer button and choose Levels in the drop-down menu.

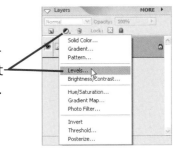

2 Click OK in the dialog box that appears and the new adjustment layer will be automatically selected in the Layers palette and the Levels dialog box will open.

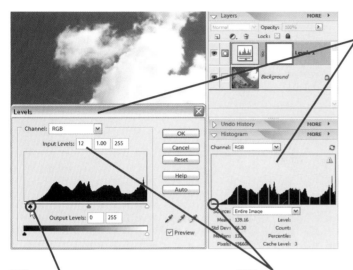

3 Reposition the Levels dialog box so that you can also see the Histogram palette, which will update as you adjust the levels.

4 Drag the black point slider right to where the Levels histogram meets the baseline.

5 Now look at the live Histogram palette and you'll see that the graph has spread to the left edge. This will remap the previous Input Level of 12 (dark gray) to black (0) and boost the photo's tonal range and contrast.

6 Remember the notion of balancing the histogram on the middle gray slider, like a see-saw? Since we've shifted the photo's overall tonal range slightly to the right, we've also bumped the gray slider slightly right as well (from 1.0 to 1.1), which slightly brightens the midtones.

Be sure to save your work when you're done.

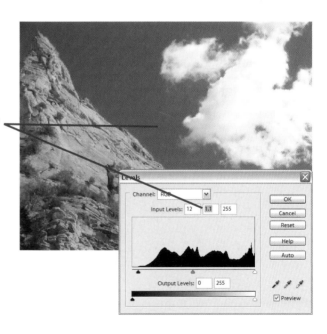

fix flashed-out areas

This photo shows one of the most common flash problems. The powdered sugar of the New Orleans beignet has been blasted by the flash, leaving little detail in the highlights. You can use an adjustment layer to fix it. (See extra bits on page 64.)

1 Open your flashed-out shot in Standard Edit mode and make sure the Layers palette appears in the Palette Bin (Window > Layers). Right-click the Background layer ([Ctrl]-click on the Mac) and choose Duplicate Layer from the drop-down menu.

2 Elements will name the duplicate Background copy; click OK to close the dialog box and the new layer will be automatically selected in the Layers palette.

3 In the Layers palette, click the Normal drop-down menu and choose Multiply.

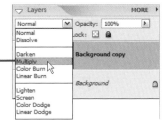

correct exposures

4 Any black in the layer is multiplied, darkening the photo overall—along with the flashed-out area. If the flashed-out area was still too bright, you could add another duplicate layer and repeat the multiply effect. Here, however, even a single duplicate layer darkens the photo too much.

5 To adjust the amount, click the Opacity drop-down menu and drag the slider to the left.

6 In this case, after a bit of trial and error, an opacity of 77 percent looks best.

7 Save the changes when you are done.

correct exposures

add fill flash

The yucca bloom photo shows what happens when you should use fill flash but forget: the foreground is too dark because the sky threw off the exposure. This too can be fixed using adjustment layers. (See extra bits on page 64.)

1 Open your photo in Standard Edit mode and make sure the Layers palette appears in the Palette Bin (Window > Layers). Right-click the Background layer (Ctrl-click on the Mac) and choose Duplicate Layer from the drop-down menu.

2 Elements will name the duplicate Background copy; click OK to close the dialog box and the new layer will be automatically selected in the Layers palette.

3 With the Background copy layer still selected, open the Levels dialog box (Ctrl L in Windows, ⌘L on the Mac).

4 Use the sliders, especially the middle gray slider, to lighten the photo. The photo will reflect the changes.

5 In the Layers palette, press Ctrl while clicking the New Layer button.

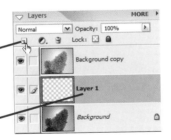

6 A new blank layer will appear between the Background and Background copy layers. For the moment, the photo will return to its original, darkened state.

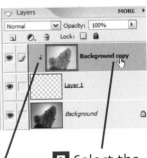

7 Select the Background copy layer again.

8 Press Ctrl G (Windows and Mac) and the Background copy layer will be grouped with the new blank Layer 1, as shown by the downward pointing arrow. By grouping the two layers, changes to one will affect the other.

correct exposures

add fill flash (cont.)

9 Press Ⓑ to select the Brush Tool in the Toolbox.

10 Set the foreground color to black.

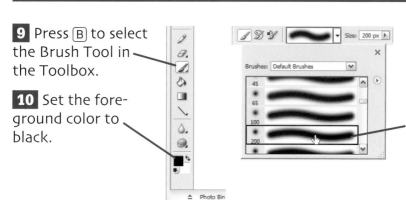

11 Use the Options Bar to select a fat brush (200-pixel diameter) with a soft, rounded tip.

12 In the Layers palette, make sure that the blank layer is selected.

13 Begin painting in the middle of the area you want lightened, which will let the previously lightened layer show through.

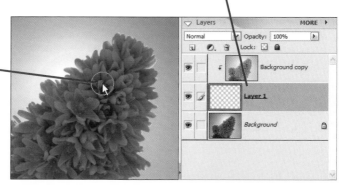

14 You need not be super careful, but try not to paint too far into the background area, which you want to remain dark.

correct exposures

15 When you're done, the middle layer will show a black area shaped like the foreground you painted out.

16 This knockout lets the Background copy show through,...

...while preserving the darker, properly exposed areas of the original Background layer.

17 Because you used a soft-edged brush, the transition from one to the other is hardly noticeable.

18 Be sure to save your changes before closing the photo.

extra bits

lighten shadows p. 45

- Stay away from using the Enhance > Adjust Lighting > Brightness/Contrast control, because its changes do not distinguish between shadows, highlights, and midtones.

- It's hard to adjust the sliders precisely. Instead, click in the number text window and use the ⬆ or ⬇ keys to change the number a digit at a time. Use Shift ⬆ or Shift ⬇ to move in 10-digit steps. The Lighten Shadows and Darken Highlights sliders also appear in the Quick Fix Lighting pane—but without the text windows.

read the histogram p. 49

- To save memory, Elements does not continuously update the histogram. If a yellow triangle appears, click it to update the histogram's display.

use levels p. 54

- Because the histogram's top-to-bottom axis reflects the amount of each value, the balance point will not always fall halfway between the right and left end points.

fix flashed-out area p. 58

- Finding the right levels often takes some trial and error. That's the great thing about adjustment layers: You can change your mind. Just double-click the adjustment layer to re-open its Levels dialog box.

add fill flash p. 60

- This layer-and-brush trick works for fixing a relatively small area in the photo. Need to lighten the entire photo? Click the Normal drop-down menu in the Layers palette and choose Screen. The steps from there are the same as fix flashed-out areas—except that it lightens instead of darkens.

4. adjust colors

Most of the time, the colors in your photos are spot on. Still, sometimes even the smartest camera gets fooled. Maybe the white balance is set for outdoors and you're inside, perhaps a flash has turned a scene cold, or nearby objects have reflected odd colors onto faces. Scanned photos or faded family shots may need some correction or rejuvenation. Before using the Standard Edit mode's color tools covered here, first try the Auto button in the Quick Fix Color palette, as explained on page 16. If you haven't already checked your monitor's settings and calibration, see pages 10–12 before digging into this chapter.

set color management

Few things are as subjective as color perception. What's deep blue to you may look purple to me. To cope with this issue, manufacturers have created numerical color profiles for every image source (your computer, scanner, camera) and color output device (monitor or printer). Using this color management feature (sometimes called an ICC profile), Elements embeds a color profile in each of your images. It's not perfect, but the idea is to keep colors from fluctuating as your photo moves from camera to monitor to Web page or snapshot.

In Standard Edit mode, press ⌐⇧Shift⌐Ctrl⌐K in Windows (⌐⇧Shift⌐⌘⌐K on the Mac) to open the Color Settings dialog box. By default, No Color Management is selected. Choose Full Color Management instead.

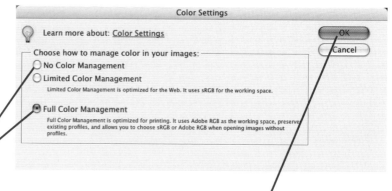

Click OK to close the dialog box and you're set. If you have a photo onscreen, you may notice an immediate, but subtle color shift.

Now, whenever you save a photo, Elements will automatically embed the chosen color profile in the file.

If you open a photo that has no color profile, Elements will ask if you want to assign it a profile. Make your choice (usually Adobe RGB), and click OK.

learn color basics

Take a minute to understand how colors are generated and you'll get a head start on how to adjust colors in photos. Three terms are used to describe how we perceive colors: Hue, Saturation, and Brightness, known as the HSB model of color. Hue is what most of us think of as color: red, yellow, blue, green are all different hues. Saturation refers to the vividness or purity of a particular color. Brightness, obviously, depends on how much light or dark a photo contains.

Whether it's on a computer screen or a printed page, a color photo never looks quite as rich as the real thing. That's because our eyes perceive a much greater range of hue, saturation, and brightness than any machine can reproduce. Your computer monitor tries to duplicate that range by mixing red, green, and blue light (using the RGB model) to generate all other colors. Printers take a stab at it by mixing pigments or inks of cyan, magenta, yellow, and black (using the CMYK model). While you might change colors for artistic reasons, the main point of adjusting colors is getting your monitor and/or printer to match the color you saw when you took the photo. To clearly show how hue, saturation, and brightness affect color, the sliders for the photos on this and the next page have been moved beyond the normal adjustment range.

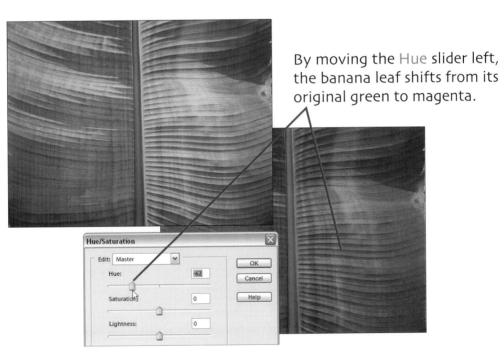

By moving the Hue slider left, the banana leaf shifts from its original green to magenta.

learn color basics (cont.)

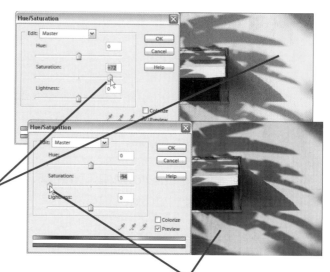

Increasing the Saturation shifts the wall's original light yellow to an orange.

Greatly decreasing the saturation, the wall becomes almost black and white.

The Lightness slider works just as you'd expect: Moving the slider right lightens the photo.

Moving the slider left darkens it.

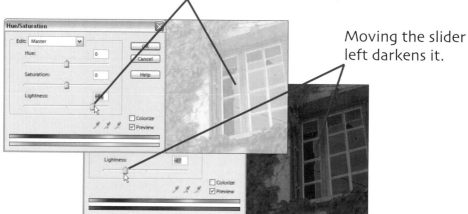

adjust colors

adjust with variations

The Color Variations feature offers a great starting point when you're still getting a feel for how hue, saturation, and brightness affect colors. It lets you compare one choice against another, making it easier to move step-by-step to the right color balance. Use this method for a while and you'll develop a good sense of how to fix a photo's color problems. (See extra bits on page 84.)

1 Open in Standard Edit mode the photo you want to fix, then from the menu bar, choose Enhance > Adjust Color > Color Variations to open the Color Variations dialog box.

2 Midtones is automatically selected, but our photo looks washed out, so we'll fix that.

3 Select Saturation and move the Amount slider left from its default middle position, just to make sure our adjustment doesn't overcorrect the saturation.

5 Examine the results and, if needed, click the More Saturation thumbnail again. You can click Undo any time to move back a step.

4 Click the More Saturation thumbnail and the After image will reflect the change.

adjust with variations (cont.)

6 Once you've fixed the saturation, reselect Midtones and click the thumbnail that seems to best correct the color (in this case, Decrease Red). You may need to click another thumbnail to fine-tune the adjustment.

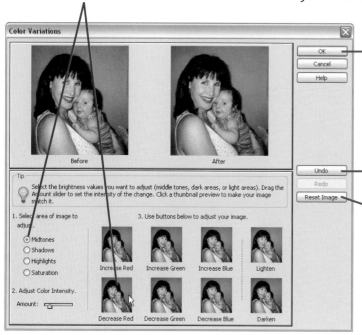

8 Once you're happy with the results, click OK to close the dialog box. Be sure to save your changes.

7 Click Undo if you want to go back a step or click Reset Image if you want to start over from the beginning.

fix hue with layer

Just as we did with levels in the previous chapter, adjustment layers can be used to change the hue, saturation, or brightness while leaving the original photo's pixels untouched. (See extra bits on page 84.)

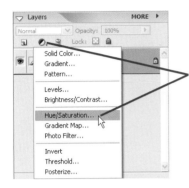

1 In Standard Edit mode, open the photo you want to fix and make sure the Layers palette appears in the Palette Bin (Window > Layers). Click the Adjustment Layer button and choose Hue/Saturation in the drop-down menu.

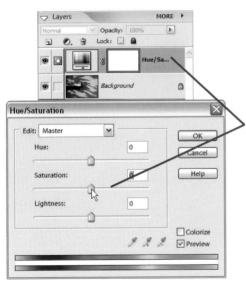

2 Click OK in the dialog box that appears and the new adjustment layer will be selected automatically in the Layers palette and the Hue/Saturation dialog box will open.

fix hue with layer (cont.)

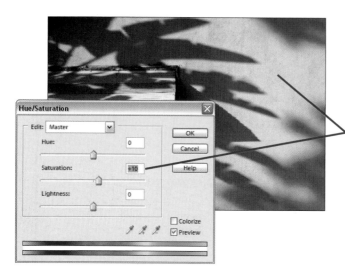

3 Click any of the three sliders or their related text windows to adjust the setting. In this case, the Saturation was boosted to +10 and the photo shows the effect.

4 To see how the change compares to the original photo, uncheck the Preview box and the photo will return to its previous color.

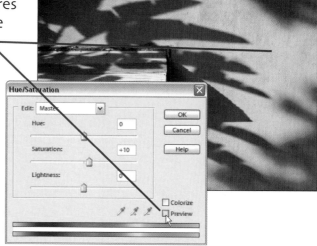

5 Recheck Preview to see the fix. Once you're satisfied with the changes, click OK to close the dialog box. Be sure to save your changes.

adjust colors

fix skin tone with mask

By creating an adjustment layer with a mask (another overlying protective layer), we can apply color fixes to just part of a photo. This is particularly useful when, as in this example, light reflecting off the nearby hydrangeas adds a pink cast to the skin tone. We used this same method to add "fill flash" on page 60. (See extra bits on page 84.)

1 Open your photo in Standard Edit mode and make sure the Layers palette appears in the Palette Bin (Window > Layers). Right-click the Background layer (Ctrl-click on the Mac) and choose Duplicate Layer from the drop-down menu.

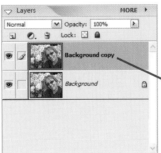

2 Elements will name the duplicate Background copy; click OK to close the dialog box and the new layer will be automatically selected in the Layers palette.

fix skin tone (cont.)

3 With the Background copy layer still selected, choose Enhance > Adjust Color > Adjust Hue/Saturation ([Ctrl][U] in Windows, [⌘][U] on the Mac).

4 When the Hue/Saturation dialog box appears, use all three sliders, if necessary, to adjust the skin tones to what looks best in the photo. Don't worry if the non-skin areas now look wrong. Click OK to close the dialog box.

adjust colors

5 In the Layers palette, press [Ctrl] while clicking the New Layer button.

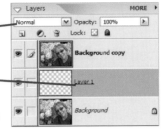

A new blank Layer 1 will appear between the Background and Background copy layers. For the moment, the photo will return to its original colors.

6 Select the Background copy layer again. Press [Ctrl][G] (Windows and Mac) and the Background copy layer will be grouped with Layer 1, as shown by the downward pointing arrow. By grouping the two layers, changes to Layer 1 will affect the Background copy layer.

7 Press [B] to select the Brush Tool in the Toolbox, set the foreground color to black by clicking the reset icon.

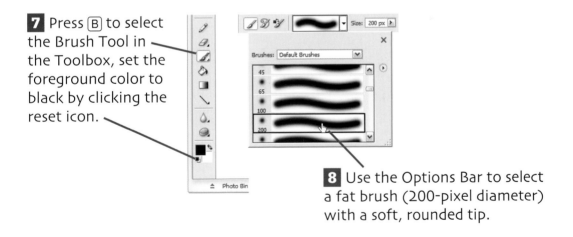

8 Use the Options Bar to select a fat brush (200-pixel diameter) with a soft, rounded tip.

fix skin tone (cont.)

9 In the Layers palette, make sure that the blank Layer 1 is selected.

10 Begin painting in the middle of the skin area.

11 When you're done, the middle layer will show a black area shaped like the area you painted out.

12 The layer mask blocks the face in the Background layer from appearing so that you only see the corrected skin tones in the Background copy.

Be sure to save your changes before closing the photo.

adjust colors

remove color cast

Sometimes a photo has a color cast in which even pure blacks and whites show a bit of color. When importing with a scanner, it's common for the photos to take on a slight blue cast.

When you compare the before and after versions, you realize how much color cast the original contains. In this case, the original has a slight blue-purple cast in the shadows. If you're not sure if a photo has a cast, give it a try since the technique's reversible.

1 Open in Standard Edit mode the photo that you suspect has a color cast. Choose Enhance > Adjust Color > Remove Color Cast to open the Remove Color Cast dialog box. The cursor becomes an eye dropper that you click in a part of the photo that's supposed to be pure white or black.

2 When you click the dropper, any color cast will disappear. If nothing happens, the photo may have no cast. If the photo gains color, you didn't click on a pure black or white spot. Click Reset if need be to start over. Once you've removed the cast—or realized the photo has none—click OK. Save your changes.

remove color noise

Sometimes photos will show a lot of splotchiness in the sky or other areas with broad patches of color, particularly when you zoom in. This splotchiness is called noise, and it's the digital equivalent of film grain. As with film, it usually appears when shooting in low light. Thankfully, in this post-film era, noise is easy to remove.

1 Open the problem photo in Standard Edit mode and, from the menu bar, choose Filter > Noise > Reduce Noise to open the Reduce Noise dialog box. The dialog box's initial settings are applied immediately but we'll adjust them in a second.

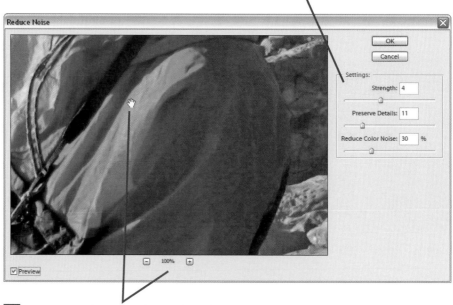

2 First use the Hand Tool and the ⊕ or ⊖ buttons to zero in on the problem area.

adjust colors

3 The trick is to reduce the noise while preserving as much detail as possible. Use the Strength, Preserve Details, and Reduce Color Noise sliders to find the best compromise.

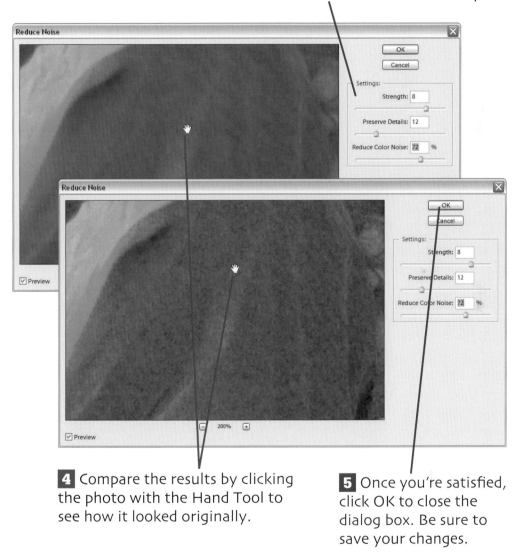

4 Compare the results by clicking the photo with the Hand Tool to see how it looked originally.

5 Once you're satisfied, click OK to close the dialog box. Be sure to save your changes.

warm or cool colors

Back in the days of film, photographers had to pay attention to whether they were shooting outdoors or indoors, and whether the lighting was incandescent

or fluorescent. Most digital cameras now have auto white balance, which handles this for you—unless you turn it off. That's one instance when you might need to warm or cool a photo's color. The example photo shows another: on a cloudy day you may need a little warmth to take the shivers off. (See extra bits on page 84.)

1 Open the problem photo in Standard Edit mode and, from the menu bar, choose Layer > New Adjustment Layer > Photo Filter. Click OK to create a new adjustment layer named Photo Filter 1 and the Photo Filter dialog box appears. By default, Elements immediately applies the Warming Filter (85) at a Density of 25 percent.

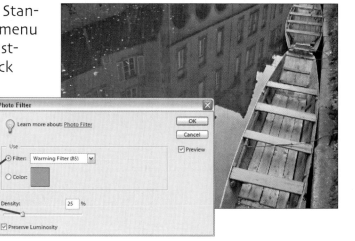

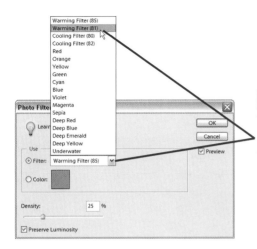

2 For this example, that seems a bit too warm, so click the Filter pop-up menu and choose Warming Filter (81), which is more subdued than Warming Filter (85). If you need to cool a photo, choose one of the two cooling filters. Cooling Filter (80) is more intense (bluer) than Cooling Filter (82).

3 Once you choose the new filter, the effect appears immediately in the photo.

4 Adjust the density if needed.

5 Once you're satisfied, click OK to apply the change and close the dialog box. Save your changes.

adjust colors

convert colors

In a world awash with color photos, sometimes you can make an image stand out by converting it to a black-and-white shot or an old-fashioned sepia-toned photo.

1 Open the photo in Standard Edit mode and, from the menu bar, choose Enhance > Adjust Color > Remove Color. The photo will convert to a grayscale image.

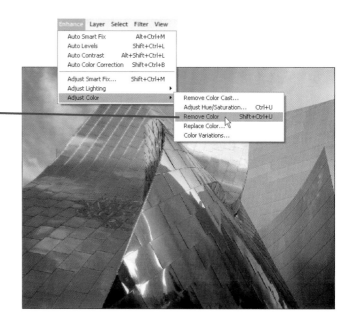

2 From the menu bar, choose Enhance > Adjust Color > Color Variations.

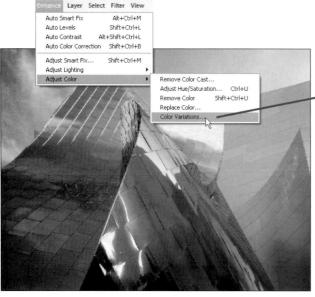

3 In the Color Variations dialog box, Midtones will already be selected.

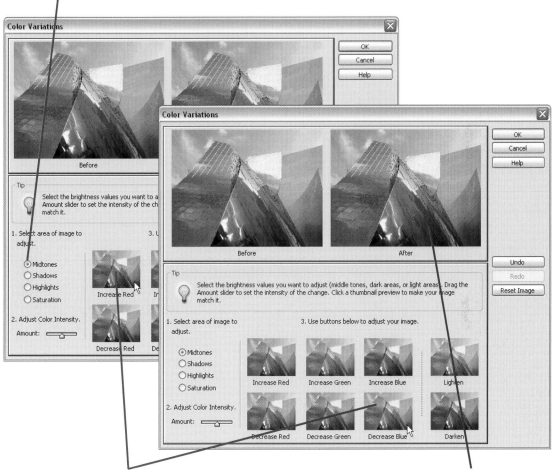

4 Click the Increase Red thumbnail, then the Decrease Blue thumbnail.

5 The now sepia-toned version will appear in the After thumbnail. Tweak the other values if you like.

6 Once you're happy, click OK to close the dialog box. Save your changes.

adjust colors

extra bits

adjust with variations p. 69

- It's common to bounce between the Midtones and Saturation choices in the Color Variations dialog box. You will seldom need to select Shadows or Highlights simply because Midtones fixes most of the color problems.
- If you have an old color print or slide that's faded over time, try boosting the saturation in the Variations dialog box to bring it back to life.

fix hue with layer p. 71

- You can readjust the hue/saturation any time by double-clicking the adjustment layer in the Layers palette.
- If you want more control, click in the number text window and use the ⬆ or ⬇ keys to change the number one digit at a time. Use [Shift]⬆ or [Shift]⬇ to move in 10-digit steps.

fix skin tone p. 73

- Once you've created the knock-out layer, you can adjust not only the color but also the exposure. Depending on which layer you select, you can apply color/lighting changes to the Background or Background copy.

warm or cool colors p. 80

- While you could apply a warming or cooling filter directly to the photo's Background layer, using the adjustment layer leaves your original pixels untouched.
- Whether you're warming or cooling a photo, feel free to readjust the Density slider from the standard 25 percent. But if you want a realistic effect, keep it below 40 percent.

adjust colors

5. repair & transform photos

Repairing photos lets you restore something similar to what used to be there. Many of the same repair tools and methods also enable you to transform photos into something not seen when you snapped the picture. Some of the repair techniques require a lot of steps, but they're worth the effort because they'll give you dramatic control over all your photos.

remove dust, scratches

Dust and scratches are a constant problem any time you scan slides or prints. While this example shows dust being removed, the same method can be used for small scratches.

Unmagnified, this slide looks fairly clean.

But when you zoom in, the light sky area is full of debris.

repair & transform photos

While Elements includes a special filter for this (Filter > Noise > Dust & Scratches), it's applied to the entire photo. You could select only the dust areas and then apply the filter, but that's too much trouble.

1 Instead, zoom in on a problem spot.

2 Select the Spot Healing Brush Tool.

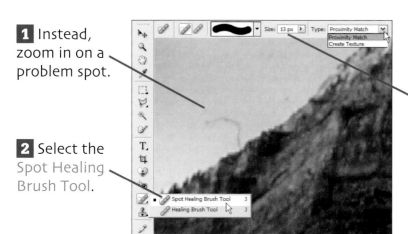

3 Use the Options Bar to pick a soft-edged brush (13 pixels is a good size) and make sure the Type is set to Proximity Match.

4 Position the brush over the dust spot (or in our example, a strand of fuzz).

5 If it's a single spot, click once. If it's a strand, as here, click and drag.

6 Release the cursor and the spot will disappear into the surrounding color.

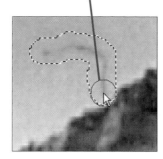

Use the Hand Tool to move to the next bit of dust and repeat the steps above until you've cleaned up all the problem areas. Save your changes.

repair & transform photos

fix blemishes

Fixing blemishes is not much different from eliminating dust spots: The Spot Healing Brush Tool is the best tool for both since you're blending a spot to match its surroundings.

1 Use the Zoom and Hand tools to get close enough to the blemish area that you can see what you're doing.

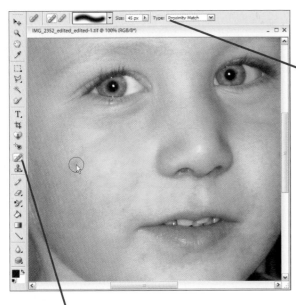

3 Use the Options Bar, pick a soft-edged brush just slightly larger than the blemish (in our example 45 pixels is a good size), and make sure the Type is set to Proximity Match.

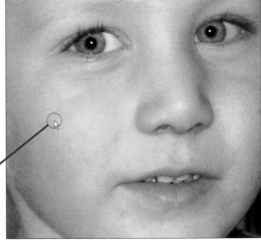

2 Select the Spot Healing Brush Tool.

4 Position the brush over the blemish and click once. The blemish will disappear as the area takes on the color of the surrounding area.

Use the Hand Tool to move to the next blemish and repeat the steps above until you've removed the most obvious spots. Save your changes.

repair & transform photos

repair areas

The Spot Healing Brush Tool performs miracles, but it has limits. Old prints, for example, often have subtle cracks in their finish, which a scanner winds up making even more apparent. The Spot Healing Brush, set to Proximity match, would duplicate any nearby cracks, making the problem worse. If set to Create Texture, it would erase the cracks—along with all the underlying pixel variation. To repair such damage while preserving the underlying texture, your best bet is the Healing Brush Tool. (See extra bits on page 116.)

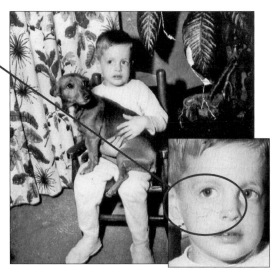

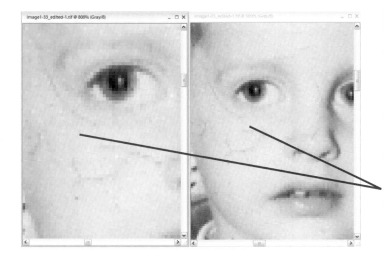

1 From the menu bar, choose View > New Window for Image, which will open a second view of the image. Use the Zoom and Hand tools to position the two windows side by side; one with a pixel-level view of the damage, the other zoomed out enough to give you an overall view of how the fix will look in the final photo.

repair areas (cont.)

2 Select the Healing Brush Tool, which shares a Toolbox berth with the Spot Healing Brush.

3 Use the Options Bar to set the brush's Diameter (fairly small, 5 pixels in our example), Hardness (23 percent is a good place to start), and leave the Mode set at Normal.

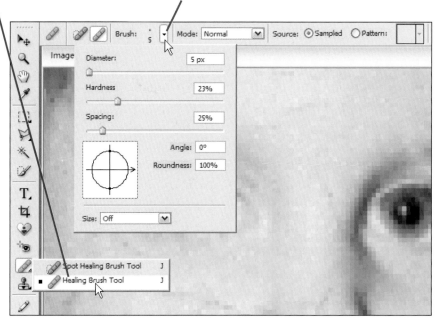

4 While pressing [Alt] in Windows ([Option] on the Mac), click the cursor in an area with the mix of light/dark pixels you want applied to the damage. (Don't worry about matching the color; the tool will perform that magic.) The cursor will turn into a cross-hair tool to help you pinpoint exactly what you're sampling. Release the cursor and [Alt] or [Option] key once you've taken the sample.

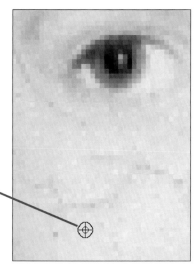

repair & transform photos

5 Position your cursor over a damaged area and click to repair it. A circle marks where the repair is being applied; a cross marks which pixels are being sampled for the fix.

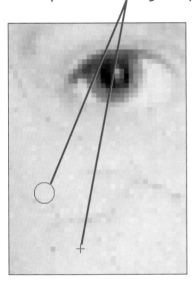

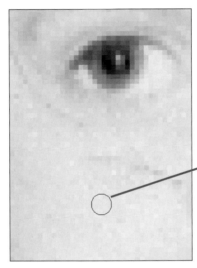

6 Continue applying the repair one click at a time, or click and drag the cursor to fix a whole line at once. When you release the cursor, it may take a second for the fix to be applied.

7 When you think you've repaired all the damaged areas, check your second zoomed-out view of the photo to be sure.

Be sure to save your changes.

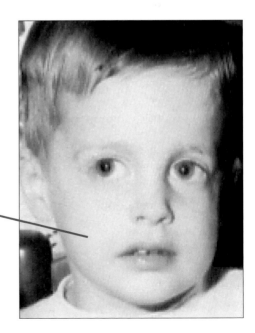

restore missing areas

If half a photo is missing, you can't recreate something from nothing. But it's surprising how often you can restore smaller missing areas using the Clone Stamp Tool to duplicate nearby areas bit by bit. In the example, we start by fixing an area of uniform color, then take on a harder-to-fix striped area. (See extra bits on page 116.)

2 Use the Options Bar to pick a small soft-tip brush. In our example, a size 9 pixel brush will work well.

1 Zoom in a bit on the easier-to-fix area and select the Clone Stamp Tool in the Toolbox.

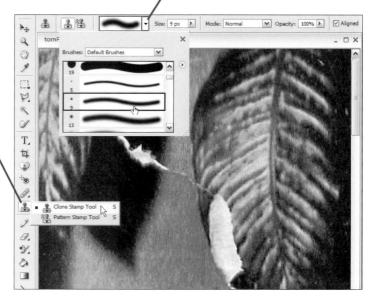

3 While pressing Alt in Windows (Option on the Mac), click the cursor near the damage to grab a similarly colored sample.

4 Release the cursor.

5 Click on the damaged area. A circle marks where the repair is being applied; a cross marks the sample source.

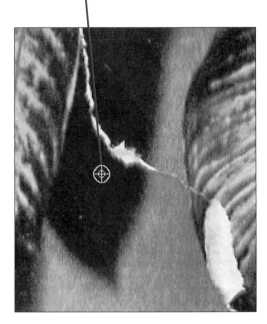

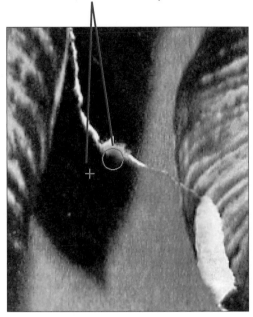

6 Continue applying the sample to the damaged area, either one click at a time or in tiny brush strokes. Resample and repeat the process for other uniformly colored areas.

restore missing areas (cont.)

7 We need to get closer to restore the striped leaf, so choose View > New Window for Image to open a second view of the image. Use the Zoom and Hand tools to position a zoomed-in view next to an overall view.

8 Use the Options Bar to pick a brush with a fuzzy tip in a larger size (21 pixels in our example).

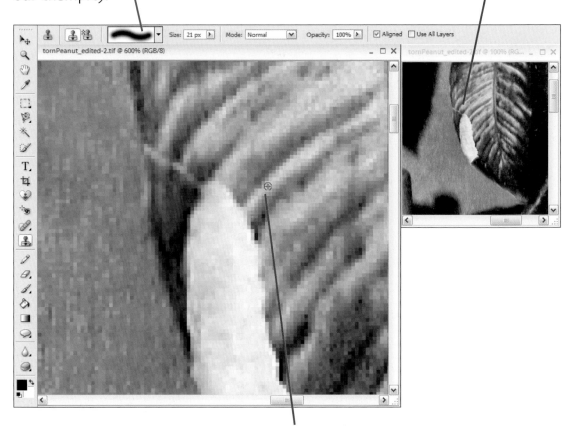

9 While pressing [Alt] in Windows ([Option] on the Mac), click the cursor in the middle of a striped leaf.

10 Release the cursor.

repair & transform photos

11 Align your brush tip with the middle of the stripe but extending into the blank area. Its reach will be indicated by a 21-pixel-wide circle—the diameter of the Clone Stamp Tool's brush. Click once and the stripe will be applied to the blank area.

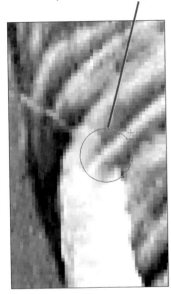

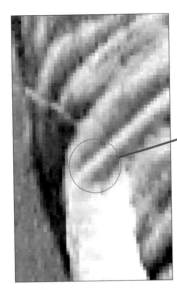

12 Use the cross marking the sample source to keep the brush aligned with the middle of the stripe. Continue painting into the blank area one click at a time. Stop short of the opposite edge of the blank area.

13 While pressing Alt in Windows (Option on the Mac), grab a sample of the next stripe.

14 Repeat the process of extending the stripe out into the blank area.

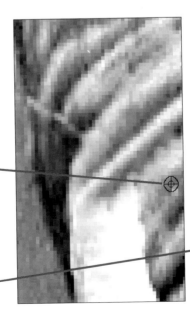

repair & transform photos

restore missing areas (cont.)

15 Once you've filled in the main area, select a smaller brush and continue using the Clone Stamp Tool to patch details along the edge.

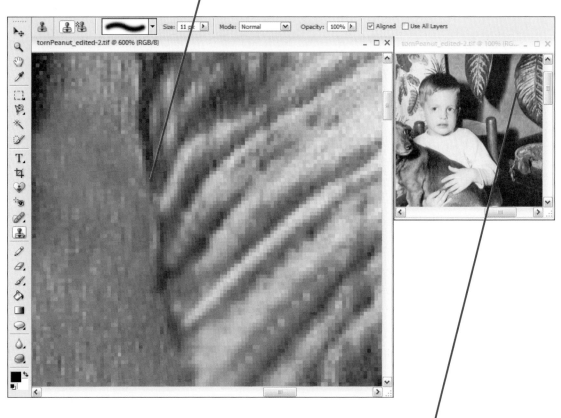

16 When you think you've repaired all the damaged areas, check the zoomed-out view to be sure.

17 Save your changes.

repair & transform photos

select part of photo

Elements offers four main tools for selecting parts of a photo—the Marquee, Lasso, Magic Wand, and Selection Brush. Once a selection's made, it can be deleted, copied, or changed without affecting the rest of the photo.

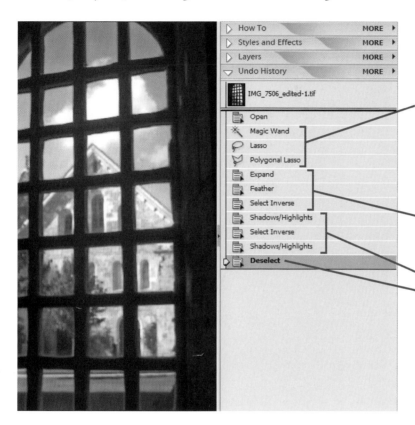

As the Undo History palette for this photo shows, it's common to use a combination of selection tools. Once you've selected an area, you then apply various commands to expand, shrink, or reverse the selection. In the typical retouching session, you then apply several fixes before finally deselecting the area. As with so much of Elements, trial and error soon shows you which tools and methods suit your style.

select part of photo (cont.)

With the circle-version of the Marquee Tool set to Fixed Aspect Ratio, it's easy to select the round logo on this German telephone booth.

You can then apply such transformations as Image > Transform > Free Transform to pivot the circle open like a window.

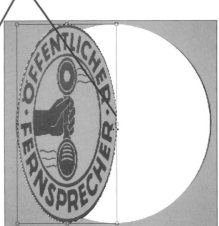

With the Magic Wand Tool set for a wide range of color (Tolerance 64) in a single area (Contiguous), you can quickly select the block of blue-purple hyacinths.

Then you can use the Shadows/Highlights dialog box to lighten only that color.

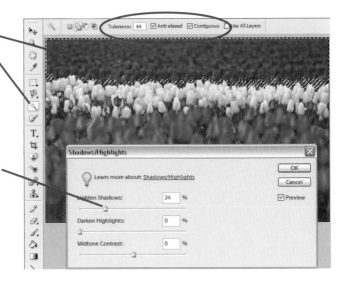

repair & transform photos

With the Selection Brush Tool set for a large brush with a very defined tip (Size 19 pixels, Hardness 100 percent), you can just brush over an area to select it. In this example of extreme red eye, however, Elements may have met its match.

All three variations of the Lasso Tool work by drawing a loop around an area to select it. While it can be as tricky to use as double-sided tape, the Magnetic Lasso works well for laying a line down along the irregular edge in the example.

repair & transform photos

modify selection

After selecting part of a photo, it's easy to modify that selection. You add to the selection or remove some of it. The Select menu lets you change the boundary between the selection and the rest of the photo.

All four selection tools let you add to your selection by using the tool while pressing Shift.

You can remove from the selection while using the tool by pressing Alt (Option on the Mac).

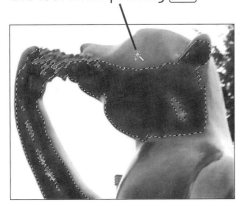

To change the boundary of a selection, choose Select > Modify and pick from the drop-down menu.

Our cookie selection with the Magnetic Lasso was a little ragged, so we choose Select > Modify > Smooth. A dialog box controls the amount of smoothing.

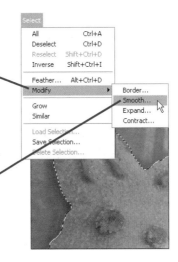

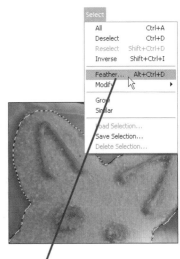

Having smoothed the selection, we want to soften its edge by choosing Select > Feather.

When you choose Select > Feather, a dialog box controls the width of the feathering in pixels.

Set to 0 pixels leaves a distinct boundary,...

...10 pixels blurs it a bit,...

...and 50 pixels creates a very soft edge.

Sometimes it's much easier to select what you don't want and then reverse the selection. To adjust the exposure outside the window, for example, would require selecting each pane of glass.

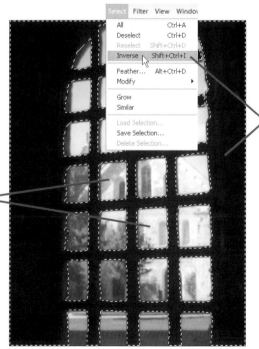

Instead, use the Magic Wand to select the surrounding black, then choose Select > Inverse.

That reverses the selection to the view outside.

repair & transform photos

remove objects

The Healing Brush and Clone Stamp examples earlier in the chapter gave you a sense of how easy it might be to remove objects in a photo. With your new selection skills, we'll start small by removing some distracting wires. (See extra bits on page 116.)

1 To ensure we don't remove any of the sign, select the sky above and below it.

2 Choose Select > Save Selection so that all your work making the selection doesn't disappear with the click of a wrong key.

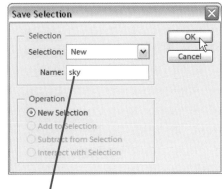

3 Name the selection and click OK to close the dialog box.

repair & transform photos

4 Choose the Clone Stamp Tool.

5 Set the brush tip small enough to work amid the wires (13 pixels is a good size), then Alt-click (Option-click on the Mac) to grab a sample of the sky. Release the cursor.

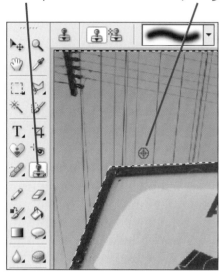

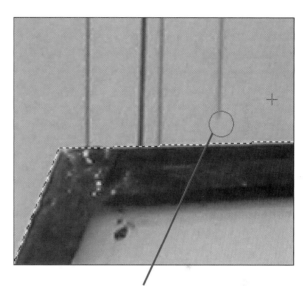

6 Start erasing the wires one click at a time. A circle marks where the stamp is applied; a cross marks the sample source. Because only the sky's selected, we can click right up to the sign without turning it blue.

remove objects (cont.)

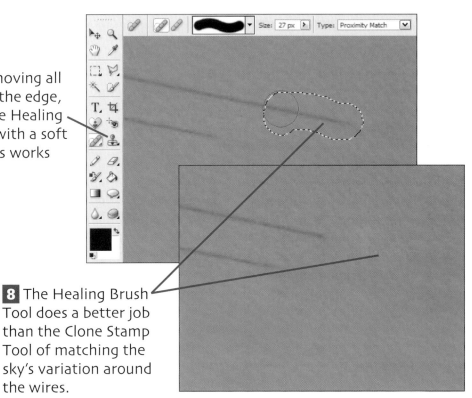

7 After removing all wires along the edge, switch to the Healing Brush Tool with a soft tip (27 pixels works well here).

8 The Healing Brush Tool does a better job than the Clone Stamp Tool of matching the sky's variation around the wires.

Though it takes time, the final photo shows no sign of the previous tangle of wires.

combine photos

Using layers, we're going to move items from one photo to another. It takes a lot of steps. But, once you master this method, you can combine bits and pieces from multiple images in a single photo. (See extra bits on page 116.)

1 Open a photo to which you want to add items from another photo. Our example is the same alterations sign we used in the previous section.

2 In the Layers palette, double-click the Background layer, marked with a lock.

3 The New Layer dialog box will name it Layer 0.

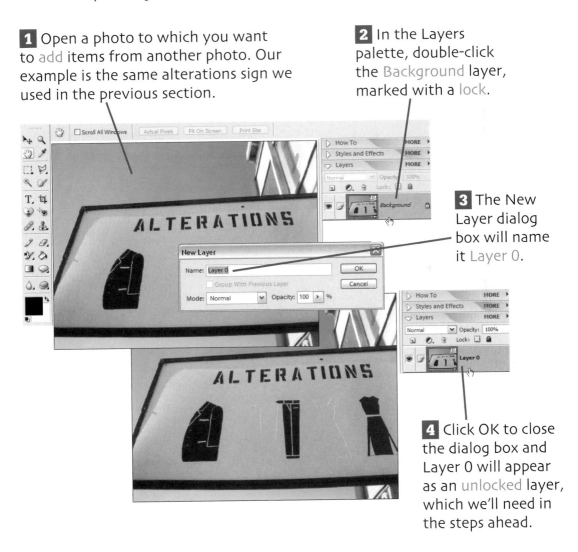

4 Click OK to close the dialog box and Layer 0 will appear as an unlocked layer, which we'll need in the steps ahead.

combine photos (cont.)

5 In remove objects, we saved the blue sky as a selection, which we can reactivate now. Choose Select > Load Selection and the Selection drop-down menu automatically lists the previously saved sky. Click OK to close the dialog box.

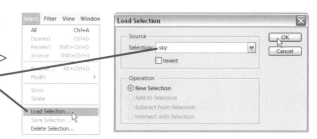

6 The reactivated selection will be marked by a dashed border.

7 Press (Delete) and the selection will disappear, leaving a checker-board area in the photo to indicate a now transparent area.

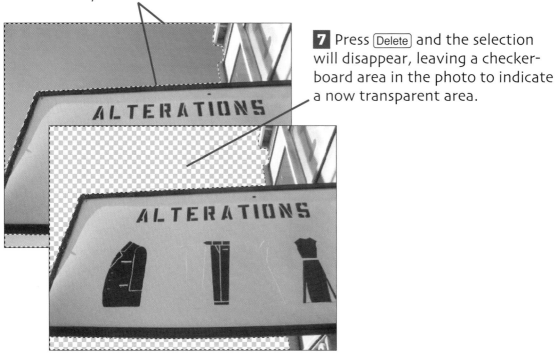

8 Switch to your second photo and select what you want to move to the first photo, in this case a more dramatic sky.

9 Choose Layer > New > Layer via Copy.

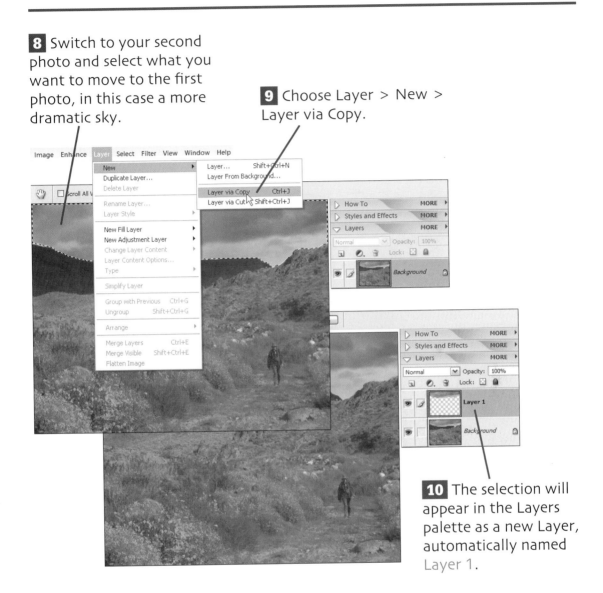

10 The selection will appear in the Layers palette as a new Layer, automatically named Layer 1.

repair & transform photos

combine photos (cont.)

11 Use the Photo Bin to bring up the still-open first photo. Position the windows so that the first photo is visible right below the second photo.

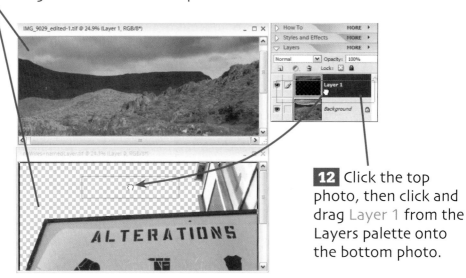

12 Click the top photo, then click and drag Layer 1 from the Layers palette onto the bottom photo.

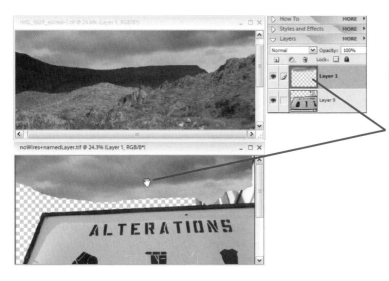

13 Release the cursor and Layer 1 will be pasted into the bottom photo. It also will appear in the Layers palette with checkerboarding marking its transparent areas. Minimize or close the other photo to give you more room to work.

repair & transform photos

14 Click the Move Tool in the Toolbox (or press V).

15 A dashed line borders the new layer, with square "handles" at its corners and sides.

16 Click and drag the various side and corner handles to fit Layer 1 over the transparent area.

17 Layer 1 is not big enough, however, to cover the area below the sign.

combine photos (cont.)

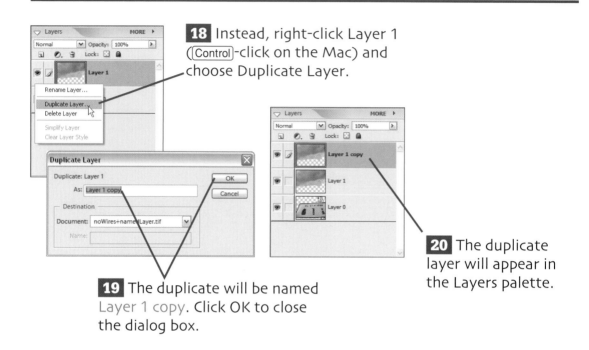

18 Instead, right-click Layer 1 (Control-click on the Mac) and choose Duplicate Layer.

19 The duplicate will be named Layer 1 copy. Click OK to close the dialog box.

20 The duplicate layer will appear in the Layers palette.

21 To see the original image, click and drag Layer 0 to the top of the Layers palette.

22 Select Layer 1 copy in the Layers palette, then click the Move Tool in the Toolbox (or press Ⓥ).

23 Use the ⬇ key to shift Layer 1 copy down enough to cover the area below the sign. (Don't click on the image or you'll wind up reselecting the visible Layer 0.) A dashed line marks the edge of the layer as it moves down the image.

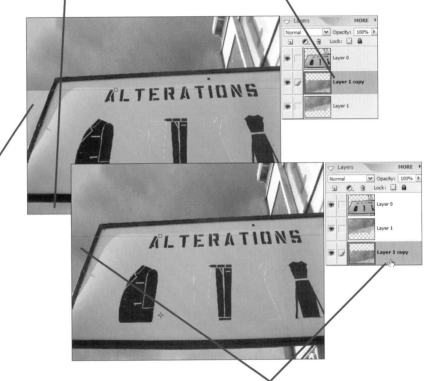

24 A bit of brighter sky mars the effect, but that's easy to fix.

25 Click and drag Layer 1 copy to the bottom of the Layers palette. This puts it beneath Layer 1, blocking out the lighter area to create a seamless new sky.

26 Merge the layers by choosing Layer > Flatten Image. Save your changes.

create a panorama

Nothing puts the viewer into a scene more dramatically than a panorama photo. Many digital cameras include features to help you create a panoramic picture by overlapping a series of photos. Elements's Photomerge feature then takes those multiple photos and stitches them into a single photo. (See extra bits on page 116.)

1 Use the File Browser to find and open the photos with which you'll build the panorama.

2 After the photos open in Standard Edit mode, position them so you can compare their exposure and color. Fix any differences now—before you start creating the panorama.

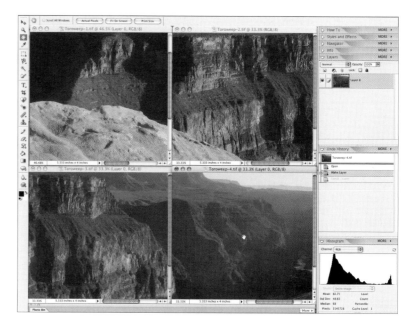

repair & transform photos

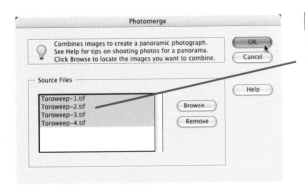

3 Choose File > New > Photomerge Panorama to open the Photomerge™ dialog box. The open photos will be listed in the dialog box, but you must select each one before clicking OK.

4 If Elements cannot merge all the photos, it puts the left-over images at the top.

5 Click and drag the first leftover photo to the correct spot in the panorama.

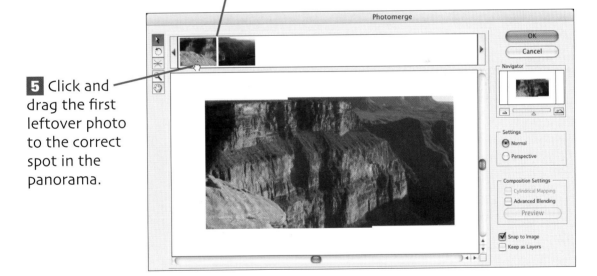

create a panorama (cont.)

6 You don't need to be that precise when you drag the image into place. It will jump into position because Snap to Image is checked by default.

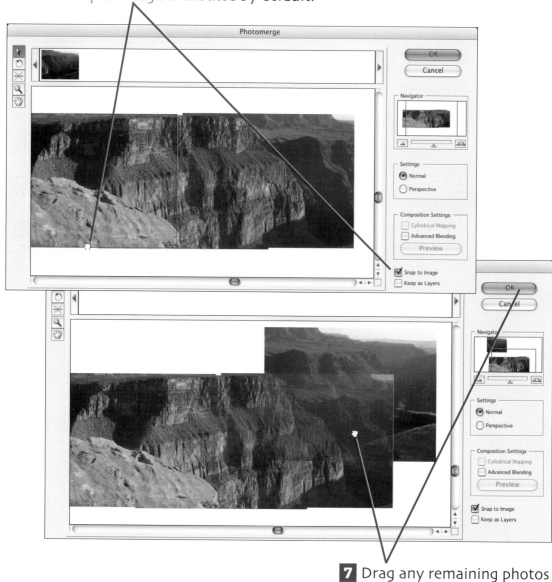

7 Drag any remaining photos into place and click OK.

repair & transform photos

8 If the original pictures were not perfectly aligned, there may be some ragged borders in the panorama image. Clean them up with the Crop Tool.

The panorama is a new file, so be sure to save your work.

extra bits

repair areas p. 89

- Think no one will notice the effects of the Spot Healing Brush compared with the Healing Brush? Our eyes instantly detect such things in faces.

- The best diameter for the Healing Brush Tool will depend on the size of the flaw. The larger the flaw, the bigger the brush.

- As you move around the photo and repair areas, use [Alt]-click ([Option]-click on the Mac) to grab new pixel samples nearer the area being fixed.

restore missing areas p. 92

- Though the example is black and white, the same steps apply working with full-color photos.

- When you change the brush size, stay with a fuzzy tip so each click/stroke blends well.

remove objects p. 102

- To paint out an object wider than the Healing Brush Tool's tip, switch to the Clone Stamp Tool. The Healing Brush tries to blend the object with the color of the surrounding area, which creates a mess.

- The same methods can add objects to a photo. It's just a matter of what you sample.

combine photos p. 105

- Unlocking the Background layer lets you change its order in the Layers palette. The layer order works like a stack of windows. Transparent portions of the upper layers let you see any layers beneath them; solid portions on top block the appearance of those below.

- To reposition the entire bounding box, click and drag the red cross-hair at its middle.

create a panorama p. 112

- Whether your camera includes an auto-stitch feature or you shoot a photo series manually, use the same exposure settings and lens length for all the photos.

- Position your panorama-destined photos to see them simultaneously in Standard Edit mode, then compare their histograms to see if any exposures need fixing.

6. share photos

The payoff for all that work fixing your photos comes when you can share them with friends and relatives. Some of them will want prints, others will prefer to see them on a computer screen. Either way, Elements makes it easy. Users of the Windows version have another option, ordering bound albums online, covered in detail in another Peachpit Press title, Creating a Photo Album in Photoshop Elements for Windows by Katherine Ulrich.

print photos

Printing photos with Elements couldn't be easier: Open the photo or photos you want to print, choose File > Print, pick a size, and click Print.

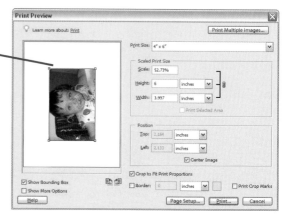

But Elements also has a less-obvious, paper-saving option called the Picture Package, which lets you print different-sized photos on a single sheet. You can use the same photo or several photos. Either way, you wind up with a photo package akin to those offered by school and wedding photographers. The Windows version is explained here; the Mac version on pages 120–121. (See extra bits on page 129.)

In the Windows version of Elements, open the photo or photos you want to print in Quick Fix or Standard Edit mode and choose File > Print Multiple Photos. In the Print Photos dialog box, your open photos run down the left.

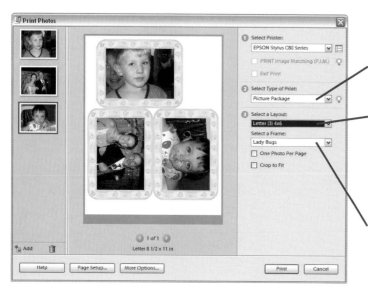

Choose Picture Package from the second drop-down menu and the center layout will reflect the choice. Use the third drop-down menu to choose a photo-layout combination. (In our example, a 4 x 6 print of three different photos will appear on a single letter-sized sheet.) If you like, you can use the fourth drop-down menu to select a fanciful frame for the photos.

share photos

If you want multiple, but different-sized, copies of the same photo, check One Photo Per Page. In our example, that change means we'll have nine 4 x 6 prints, with the first photo on the first sheet.

If you're printing multiple sheets, click the arrows to see the other sheets. Here, the second sheet shows three 4 x 6s of the second photo. Once you've set your combination, click Print.

print photos (cont.)

In the Mac version of Elements, open the photo or photos you want to print in Quick Fix or Standard Edit mode and choose File > Picture Package. In the Picture Package dialog box, set the Use drop-down menu to Open Files.

Set your paper size and the layout you want with the second and third drop-down menus. Make sure Resolution is set to at least 150. By default, each layout prints multiple sizes of the same photo. When you're done, click OK.

To mix different photos in the same layout, click any photo in the layout.

You can then browse to select the photos already open (or unopened ones), which will then replace the original in the layout. We've done just that for two photos in the layout. When you're done, click Print.

A flurry of windows will appear and disappear as the Picture Package is generated. In a few moments, each page of the package will appear,...

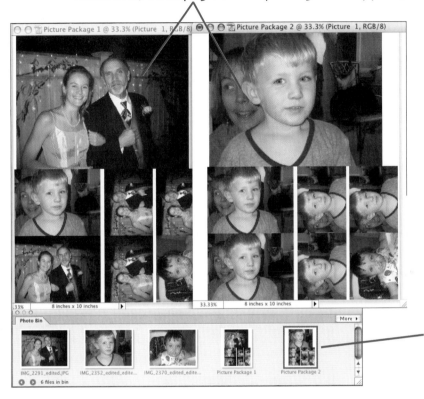

...along with a thumbnail in the Photo Bin.

Print each one individually and save them for later use if you like. If closed without being saved (⌘S), they will disappear and not print.

email photos

For convenience, nothing beats email for sharing photos. Elements makes it even easier by automatically creating a compact JPEG version of your photo while maintaining the larger original.

1 In the Windows version of Elements, if you haven't already set your email preferences in the Organizer, you still can reach them from the Editor. Choose Edit > Preferences > Organize & Share.

2 Select E-mail, then choose an E-mail client from the drop-down menu.

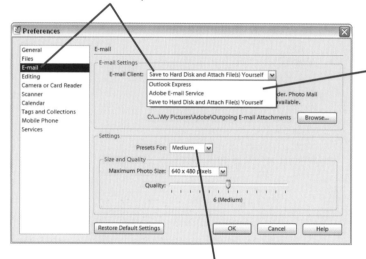

3 If you choose Outlook Express, Elements will automatically attach photos to a blank outgoing message. Adobe E-mail Service creates a message that's sent by Elements itself. The Save to Hard Disk choice stores the converted photo on your computer for sending manually with any email program.

4 By default, the photo will be converted to a Medium 640 x 480 pixel photo. Use the drop-down menu if you want to change the setting, then click OK to close the dialog box.

share photos

5 After setting the preferences, open the photo(s) you want to send and choose File > Attach to Email. Elements will switch to its Organizer.

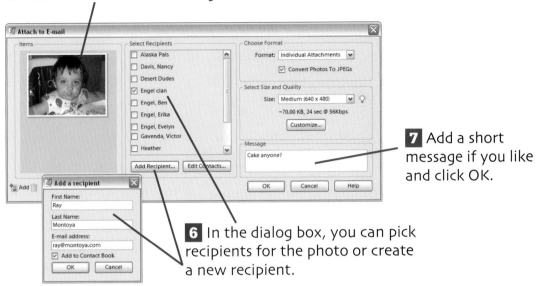

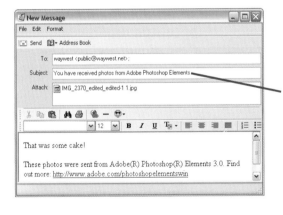

7 Add a short message if you like and click OK.

6 In the dialog box, you can pick recipients for the photo or create a new recipient.

8 The message with the attached photo will appear in the email client you set in Preferences. In this example, Elements handles the message. You may want to change the default subject line to something more personal.

9 Click Send and you're done.

share photos

email photos (cont.)

1 In the Mac version of Elements, open the photo(s) you want to send by email and choose File > Attach to Email.

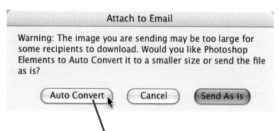

2 When Elements asks if it can send a smaller file, click Auto Convert, which will create a medium-sized (640 x 480 pixels) copy in the space-saving JPEG format.

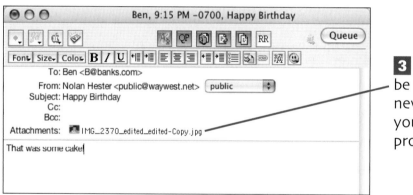

3 The photo will be attached to a new message in your default email program.

4 Once you manually add a recipient, subject line, and text, send the message.

save for the web

Posting photos on a Web page is a great way to share them. When you make prints, you try to preserve every last detail to get the most faithful photo reproduction. But when you prepare an image for the Web, it's almost the opposite: You try to slim the file down so it will download quickly to the viewer's computer. The slimming process is called optimizing, and Elements's Save For Web dialog box makes it easy. (See extra bits on page 129.)

1 Open the photo you want to use on the Web in Quick Fix or Standard Edit mode and choose File > Save for Web. The photo will appear in the Save For Web dialog box.

2 By default, the photo opens at 100 percent, so use the Hand Tool to maneuver the main part of your photo into view.

3 Set the Preset drop-down menu to JPEG Medium.

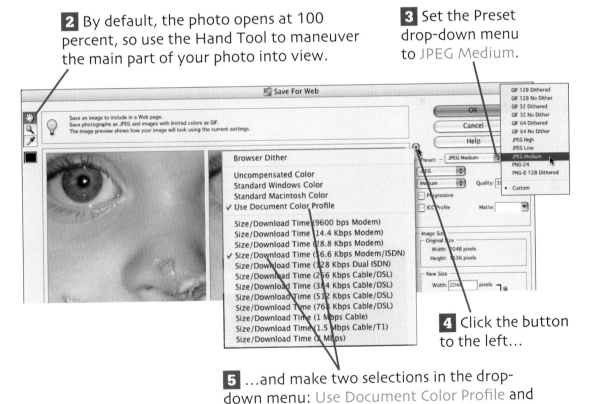

4 Click the button to the left...

5 ...and make two selections in the drop-down menu: Use Document Color Profile and Size/Download Time (56.6 Kbps Modem/ISDN).

save for the web (cont.)

6 Check two more boxes:
Progressive and ICC Profile.

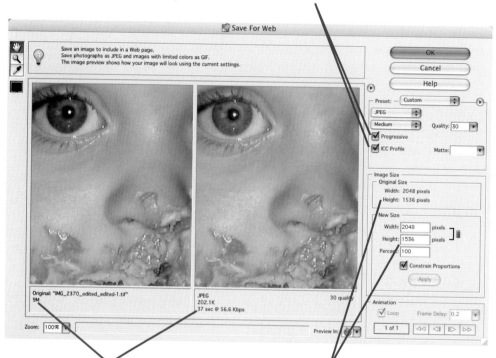

7 Listed at the bottom left is the photo's present size in the TIFF format (in this case 9 megabytes). To the right is its size (202.1 bytes) as a JPEG file and how long it would take to download (37 seconds at 56.6 Kbps) if we click OK.

8 But wait, even though the format's different, the dimensions of the original and the new version remain the same: 2048 x 1536. Since the new version is going to be on a Web page, it could be a lot smaller. Otherwise, you'll wind up with a giant screen-filling photo, like this cake fan's face.

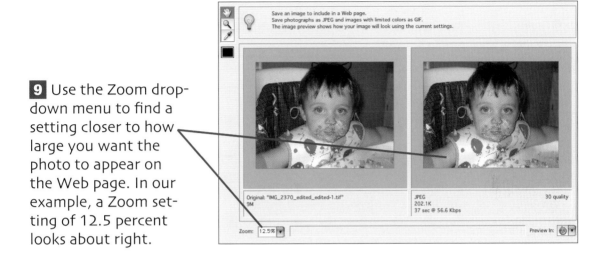

9 Use the Zoom drop-down menu to find a setting closer to how large you want the photo to appear on the Web page. In our example, a Zoom setting of 12.5 percent looks about right.

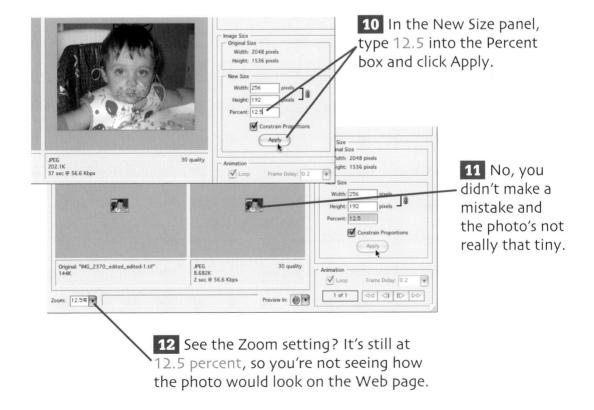

10 In the New Size panel, type 12.5 into the Percent box and click Apply.

11 No, you didn't make a mistake and the photo's not really that tiny.

12 See the Zoom setting? It's still at 12.5 percent, so you're not seeing how the photo would look on the Web page.

share photos

save for the web (cont.)

13 Set the Zoom level back to 100 percent and you can see exactly how big the photo will appear on the Web.

14 The New Size panel lists its physical dimensions at 256 x 192 pixels. That's 3.5 x 2.6 inches—just about right for viewing on a computer screen.

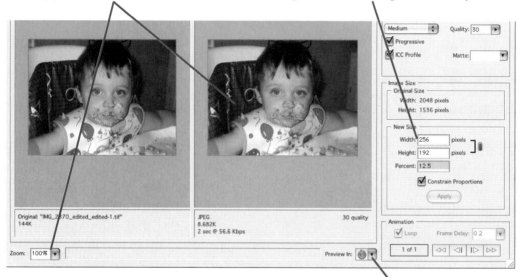

15 If you're still skeptical, click the Preview In button. Your Web browser will launch and show how the photo will look on the Web.

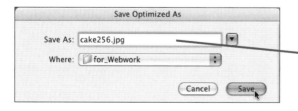

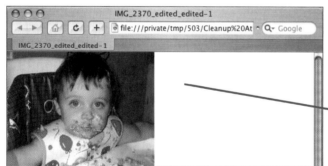

16 Click OK to save the optimized image. Name it, pick where to store it, and click Save. It will not affect your original photo. You'll need a Web program to upload the new image.

share photos

extra bits

print photos p. 120

- If the Print Preview dialog box warns that the image will print at less than 220 dpi (dots per inch), the printer probably is still set to print letter-sized documents. Choose File > Page Setup and in the Page Setup dialog box click the Printer and then Properties buttons (Windows) or use the Format for and Paper Size drop-down menus (Mac) to check and change the settings.

- The Mac Picture Package dialog box initially only shows one photo even if you've opened multiple photos.

save for the web p. 127

- You can trim so much digital fat from a Web-bound photo because of the difference between printers and computer monitors. For a print to look good, printers need to lay down at least 150 dots per inch (dpi). Photos on a monitor, however, look great at just 72–96 dpi. For onscreen Web pages, the rest of those dots can be tossed, during optimization.

- Your Size/Download Time choice doesn't change the photo in any way. It simply helps you gauge how long a viewer will have to wait to see your image.

- Choosing Progressive in the Save For Web dialog box helps Web surfers with slow connection speeds see a sketchy version of the photo as it downloads. That way they can decide if they want to wait for the whole picture or move on to another page.

- Choosing ICC in the Save For Web dialog box embeds color profile data in the photo—making it easier for other profile-enabled computers to display the photo properly.

- If anyone tried to print out the Web image of the baby's face, it would be postage-stamp size. That's the difference between the resolution of a computer screen (72dpi) and a photo print (150–300 dpi). To post photos for prints, use your Web-site creation software to create a separate download link to the big original file.

index

A

adjust color, see colors
adjust lighting, see lighting
Adobe Gamma dialog box, 11
Adobe Photo Downloader, 22
Adobe Photoshop Elements 3, vii
    computer requirements, vii
Apple menu commands, System
    Preferences, 10
arrange
    File Browser, 4
    workspaces, 7–9
Attach to Email command (File
    menu), 123
automatic sharpening, 40–41

B

binocular button, 3, 5
black and white photos, converting
    from color, 82–83
blemishes, repairing photos, 88

C

calibrating monitors, 11–12
cameras, importing photos, 14–15
card readers, importing photos, 14–15
casts, colors, 77–78
circling arrows buttons, File Browser, 3
Clone Stamp Tool, 92
collapsing
    Palette Bin, 7, 21
    Photo Bin, 7
Color pane, 38–39
Color quality panel, 10
Color Settings dialog box, 66
Color Variations dialog box, 69–70, 83
colors, 65
    Adjust Color command (Enhance
        menu), 74
    basics, 67–68
    converting, 82–83
    cooling, 80–81, 84
    correction tools, ix

fixing, 38–39
    hues with layers, 71–72, 84
    skin tones, 73–76
management, 66
removing cast, 77–78
setting monitor, 10
skin tones, 73–76
variations, 69–70, 84
warming, 80–81, 84
Colors drop-down menu, 10
combining photos, 105–111, 116
companion Web site, vii
computer requirements, running
    Adobe Photoshop Elements 3, vii
contrast reduction, 52–53
Control Panel command (Start
    menu), 10
convert colors, 82–83
cooling colors, 80–81, 84
Creating a Photo Album in Photoshop
    Elements for Windows, 117
Crop Tool, 29
cropping photos, 29–30
CRT monitor calibrating, 21
Custom command (Sort menu), 21

D

Details command (View menu), 21
Display Calibrator Assistant, 12
Display pane, 10
distorted skin tones, ix
drop-down menus, folder naviga-
    tion, 3
dust, repairing photos, 86–87

E

Edit menu commands, Preferences, 22
Elements Editor, 1, 6
email photos, 122–124
Enhance menu commands
    Adjust Color, 74
    Adjust Lighting, 45
exposures, 43
    contrast reduction, 52–53
    darken highlights, 47

flash
    adding fill, 60–63
    fixing flash-out areas, 58–59
histograms, 49–51
levels
    adjusting, 54–55
    layers, 56–57
midtone adjustments, 48
shadows/highlights, 45–47, 52, 54
Undo History palette, 44

F

Feather command (Select menu), 100
File Browser, 3–5
    importing photos, 13
    menus, 21
File menu commands
    Attach to Email, 123
    Import, 16
    Open, 14
    Page Setup, 129
    Picture Package, 120
    Print, 118
    Print Multiple Photos, 118
    Save As, 20
    Save for Web, 125
fill flash, 60–63
Filter menu commands, Noise, 78
flash
    adding fill, 60–63
    fixing flash-out areas, 58–59
    lighten entire photo, 64
fixing
    blemishes, 88
    dust/scratches, 86–87
    colors, see colors
    exposures, see exposures
    lighting, see exposures
    red eye, see red eye
folders
    importing photos, 13
    navigation, 3
    searching, 5
Folders pane, File Browser, 3
Folders tab, 4
formatting photos, 20, 122, 124,
    125–128

G

General Fixes pane, 31
getting photos
    from camera, 14–15
    from folders, 13
    from iPhoto, 19
    from Organizer, 18
    from scanner, 16–17

H

Hand Tool, 30
Healing Brush Tool, 89–91, 102,
    104, 116
heirloom photos, ix
hide/show, Palette and Photo bins, 7–9
highlights, darkening, 47
Histogram command (Window
    menu), 49
histograms, 49–51, 64
Hoeschen, Craig, xii
Hue/Saturation dialog box, 74
hue controlling, ix, 67, 68 71–72,
    74, 84

I

Image menu commands
    Rotate, 42
    Transform, 98
Import command (File menu), 16
importing photos
    from camera, 14–15
    from folders, 13
    from iPhoto, 19
    from Organizer, 18
    from scanner, 16–17
Inverse command (Select menu), 101
iPhoto
    editing with Elements, 19
    importing photos from, 19

J

JPEG files, 20
JPG files, 20

L

layers
    adding fill flash, 60–63
    fixing flashed-out areas, 58–59
    fixing hues, 71–72
    levels, 56–57
Layers command (Window menu), 58
LCD monitor calibrating, 21

levels
    adjusting, 54–55
    layers, 56–57
Levels dialog box, 54
lighting
    Adjust Lighting command
        (Enhance menu), 45
    fixing, 35–37, 45–63
    matching, 34
Lighting pane, 34–37
Load Selection command (Select
    menu), 106

M

Macintosh
    Adobe Photoshop Elements 3
        requirements, vii
    calibrating monitors, 12
    hide/show Palette Bin, 8
    hide/show Photo Bin, 7
    File Browser, 3–5
    importing photos
        from camera, 14
        from iPhoto, 19
        from scanner, 16
    setting monitor colors, 10
    Welcome screen, 2, 21
Magic Wand tool, 97–99
main windows, File Browser, 3
managing colors, 66
Marquee Lasso tool, 97–99
masks, fixing skin tones, 73–76
match lighting, 34
Metadata pane, File Browser, 3
midtones, adjusting, 48
Modify command (Select menu), 100
monitors
    calibrating, 11–12
    color setting, 10
    self-calibrating, 21

N

New Window for Image command
    (View menu), 89
Noise command (Filter menu), 78

O

objects, removing, 102–104
Open command (File menu), 14
Open File for Editing button, 2
Options Bar, Elements Editor, 6
Organizer
    disabling Photo Downloader, 22

importing photos, 18
    camera, 15
    scanner, 17
Photo Browser, 42
Windows shortcuts bar, 1

P

Page Setup command (File menu), 129
Page Setup dialog box, 129
Palette Bin
    hide/show, 8, 21
    Quick Fix mode, 6
Palette pane, details, 9
panes, rearrangement, 4
panoramas, ix, 112–116
Photo Bin, 6
    hide/show, 7
Photo Browser, 42
Photo Downloader, 22
Photo Filter dialog box, 80
Photomerge dialog box, 113
photos
    cropping, 29–30
    importing
        from camera, 14–15
        from folders, 13
        from iPhoto, 19
        from Organizer, 18
        from scanner, 16–17
    reformatting, 20
    rotating, 24–25, 42
Photoshop Elements 3, require-
    ments, vii
Photoshop Elements 3 for Windows
    and Macintosh: Visual Quickstart
    Guide, xii
Picture Package command (File
    menu), 120
Preferences command
    Edit menu, 22
    iPhoto menu, 19
Preferences dialog box, 19
Preview pane, File Browser, 3
Print command (File menu), 118
Print Multiple Photos command
    (File menu), 118
printing photos, 118–121, 129
Pupil Size drop-down menu, 28

Q

Quick Fix mode, 23
    Auto Levels button, viii
    automatic sharpening, 40–41
    colors, 38–39
    cropping, 29–30

index

Quick Fix mode (cont.)
   Elements Editor, 6
   lighting
      fixing, 35–37
      matching, 34
   red eye, 26–28
   rotating photo, 24–25
   shortcuts bar, 1
   Smart Fix, 31–33
Quick Fix palette, 6

R

RAW format, 22
rearranging panes, 4
red eye, viii, 26–28, 42
Red Eye Removal tool, 27
reducing contrast, 52–53
Reduce Noise dialog box, 78
reformatting photos, 20
Remove Color Cast dialog box, 77
removing objects, 102–104
repairing photos
   blemishes, 88
   damaged areas, 89–91, 116
   dust and scratches, 86–87
   modifying selection, 100–101
   removing objects, 102–104, 116
   restore missing areas, 92–96, 116
   selection tools, 97–99
requirements, running Adobe
   Photoshop Elements 3, vii
restoring photos
   blemishes, 88
   damaged areas, 89–91, 116
   dust and scratches, 86–87
   modifying selection, 100–101
   removing objects, 102–104, 116
   restore missing areas, 92–96, 116
   selection tools, 97–99
rotating photos, 24–25, 42

S

saturation, ix, 67–72, 74, 84
Save As command (File menu), 20
Save for Web, 125
Save Selection command (Select
   menu), 102
saving for Web, 125–129
scanners
   importing photos, 16–17, color
      cast, 77–78
scratches, repairing photos, 86–87
Search dialog box, 5
Search Results, File Browser, 5
Select menu commands
   Feather, 100

Inverse, 101
Load Selection, 106
Modify, 100
Save Selection, 102
Selection Brush tool, 97, 99
selection tools, 97–99
self-calibrating monitors, 21
sepia-toned photos, converting from
   color, 82–83
shadows
   lightening, 45–46
   sliders, 64
Shadows/Highlights dialog box,
   45–47, 52, 54
sharing photos, 117
   email, 122–124
   printing, 118–121, 129
   saving for Web, 125–129
Sharpen pane, automatic sharpening,
   40–41
shortcuts bars, Elements editor, 1
skin, blemishes, 88, fixing tones, ix,
   73–76, 84
Smart Fix, 31–33
Sort menu commands, Custom, 21
Spot Healing Brush tool, 87–89,
   90, 116
Standard Edit mode, viii
   color adjustments, see colors
   cropping, 29–30
   Elements Editor, 6
   exposures
      contrast reduction, 52–53
      darken highlights, 47
      histograms, 49–51
      midtone adjustments, 48
      shadow lightening, 45–46
   flash
      adding fill, 60–63
      fixing flash-out areas, 58–59
   levels adjustment, 54–57
   red eye, 26–28
   rotating photo, 24–25
   shortcuts bar, 1
Standard Edit palette, 6
Start menu commands, Control
   Panel, 10
System Preferences command (Apple
   menu), 10

T

Temperature tool, ix
thumbnails, Photo Bin, 6
TIFF files, 20
TIFF Options dialog box, 20
Toolbox, Elements Editor, 6
tools, color correction, ix

Transform command (Image
   menu), 98
transforming photos
   combining photos, 105–111, 116
   damaged areas, 89–91, 116
   modifying selection, 100–101
   removing objects, 102–104, 116
   restore missing areas, 92–96, 116
   selection tools, 97–99
trash button, File Browser, 3

U

Ulrich, Katherine, 117
Undo History command (Window
   menu), 44
Undo History palette, 44

V

VGA Display dialog box, 10
View menu commands
   Details, 21
   File Browser, 3
   New Window for Image, 89

W

warming colors, 80–81, 84
Web
   companion site, vii
   sharing photos, 125–129
Welcome screen, 2, 21
Window menu commands
   Histogram, 49
   Layers, 58
   Undo History, 44
Windows
   Adobe Photoshop Elements 3
      requirements, vii
   calibrating monitors, 11
   disabling Photo Downloader, 22
   File Browser, 3–5
   hide/show
      Palette Bin, 8, 21
      Photo Bin, 7
   importing photos
      cameras, 15
      scanner, 17
   setting monitor colors, 10
   shortcuts bar, 1
   Welcome screen, 2, 21
workspaces, arrangement, 7–9

Z

Zoom tool, red eye, 26